Praise for "A page from a CEO's Diary"

"Howard has always been a student of leadership. This book proves that he has learned his lessons well..."

-Richard Peddie, Chairman/CEO, MLS+E

"Howard Breen offers a compelling, no-nonsense approach to achieving success and bottom-line results. **A page from a CEO's Diary** *is a practical guide with useful exercises to ensure success. An amazing opportunity to learn and grow from his incredible talents. A must-read for leaders across all industries..."*

-Robert Leonidas, President/CEO, Nestle Canada Inc.

"A wonderful and insightful compendium of practical knowledge based on Howard's many years of real-life experience as a world-class CEO and a successful business career before that..."

-John Gustuvson, President/CEO, CMA

"A page from a CEO's Diary *is an interesting, honest and potentially life-changing account. Howard's words inspire, stimulate self-reflection and offer practical advice for career and life. This book keeps the reader continually engaged. I commend Howard—one of our country's most successful business leaders—on serving as his "brother's keeper" by sharing his vast experience and learnings to benefit others..."*

-Tony Gagliano, Chairman/CEO, St. Joseph Communications

"This is not a stodgy, anal retentive text about the abc's of business management. It is an often uncomfortably personal account of what it takes to thrive. Equal parts chess master and therapist, a CEO needs to know when to be empathetic and when to show a certain pitiless resolve. Mr. Breen shows how it's done in the real world. It ain't pretty but boy it's exhilarating..."

-John Farquhar, President, Wild Mouse Advertising

"'I view persistence as the most vital of all attributes in my career success'...This is the Howard Breen I know. But at the same time he couples this with a high level of open mindedness—an attribute not often seen in a person as focused as he is. That is why his advice on orchestrating careers, moving outside your comfort zone, and finding success will resonate so deeply with the reader. His focus on integrity is evidenced in his behavior as well as his words. He is a highly motivated person who has given the next generation of CEO's a very practical, helpful, but easily readable self help book. It is a very enjoyable read..."

-Brent Belzberg, President/CEO Torquest Partners

"From small town kid to big city executive and everything in-between... Howard has been there. **A page from a CEO's Diary** is provocative, frequently controversial but always entertaining. The lessons are universal. Howard shoots straight from the hip and invites the reader to think about their past, but more importantly to focus on their future..."

-Michael McKelvey, Partner, Borden Ladner Gervais LLP

"Powerful and honest: **A page from a CEO's Diary** provides straightforward, invaluable advice. Whether you are just beginning your career, midway through, or in the latter stages, Howard Breen's sage counsel is a wake-up call designed to positively impact your personal and business relationships, while helping you to achieve your goals. The opportunity to learn from such a dynamic, high-powered executive, as he shares his life experiences with such candor, grace, and humor is irresistible..."

-Randy Powell, President, The Armstrong Group

"A reference manual for career and personal development: Breen reveals insights based upon his own experiences and achievements. He guides readers through self assessment and then offers informed, sage, step-by-step advice. This book could change your life..."

-Larry Organ, Chairman/CEO, ConsumerBase USA

"A page from a CEO's Diary *is the perfect book to read after your last day in school and before your first real job...or for anyone who needs a refresher on finding that elusive balance between life and career..."*

-Jacques Duval, Chairman/CEO, Marketel

"Howard is a great story teller and I can hear his voice in these pages. True to form, he has generously shared them now in this very readable and memorable book. His advice on life and work is filled with good ideas, humor, a combination of insight and common sense, and best of all, lots of "Breenisms"...."

-Daryl Aitken, President, Dashboard Communications

AuthorHouse™
1663 Liberty Drive, Suite 200
Bloomington, IN 47403
www.authorhouse.com
Phone: 1-800-839-8640

First published by AuthorHouse 2/5/2009

ISBN: 978-1-4389-3781-6 (sc)
ISBN: 978-1-4389-3782-3 (hc)

Printed in the United States of America
Bloomington, Indiana

This book is printed on acid-free paper.

A page from a CEO's Diary

Howard Breen

authorHOUSE®

Dedication:

This book is dedicated to my parents for their unselfish and loving investment in all of our futures; and, to my wife Martha, our daughter Rosalind, and our son Christian...all of whom make my life a joy.

Giving Back:

It may not prove overly fruitful, but for the next two years, all net proceeds of this book will be donated in equal parts to Camp Oochigeas and PrevNet. "Ooch" is an incredible camp that brings dignity, camaraderie, laughter and hope to youngsters battling cancer. PrevNet is a non-for-profit Canadian organization founded by Doctors Debra Peplar and Wendy Craig to help bring our children into a "World without Bullying."

If you'd like to learn more about either organization please go to:

www.campooch.org

www.prevnet.ca

Forward

I readily admit I am a very lucky man. I have had a (surprisingly) successful and (fortunately) lucrative 30+ year career both in Canada, and the USA. Happily married to my best friend, we have been blessed with two outstandingly bright, loving and compassionate children. When I'm not fulfilling the role as the CEO of one of Canada's largest and pre-eminent Advertising and Communications Agencies, I tackle marathons, scuba dive, golf and ski. I also sit as a Director on numerous business and charitable boards.

Having just completed my 3rd decade in the business world, I cobbled together an openly candid book of the most important lessons I have learned about business, society, politics, family and love. I entitled this book, **"A page from a CEO's Diary."** These lessons have helped me to win more than my fair share in the game of life. By providing you with observations, anecdotes and by posing questions, I intend to challenge you to (re)evaluate your own thinking, values and practices. My hope is to help you gain a more honest picture of yourself, and what you believe. Through this, it will then be possible for you to understand what you need to do to become the best person you can be. **"A page from a CEO's Diary,"** contains the best lessons I know.

For decades, clients, friends, employees, and business associates have sought my counsel for issues they were facing. Almost to a person, each has told me to write down and publish "my advice to them" for others to be able to share. That's what I've done.

Please enjoy, **"A page from a CEO's Diary."**

-Howard J. Breen September, 2008

Contents

IV) About your family and friends

V) Issues of time/fatigue/money/jerks

VI) The world needs your best

Chapter 1

"The life unexamined is not worth living..."

-Socrates

I'm going to begin this book with the most fundamental of statements. **You'll never be truly happy with anyone or successful at anything until you are fully comfortable in your own skin.** The stability and happiness you realize in your relationships and the success you achieve in your career depend most critically on one major factor: Your ability to figure yourself out, and make sure you *are* someone you like and admire. I believe this is the entire crux of the game and something that most people don't understand. It's not about how much money you have and it's certainly not about whether you look like Brad Pitt or Halle Berry. Although admittedly, having those two things would be great. It's not whether you have the brains of Albert Einstein, or the magnetic personality and incredible abilities of a Bill Clinton.

It's really very simple. *You need to like and admire the person you are inside.* Everything else you do or think in life will come from this. Until you like and admire yourself, you will never feel fulfilled, or at peace.

I don't think a lot of people really know who they are so they can't fully like, or admire who they are. They've never taken the time to sit down and **understand all the *influences* that shaped them in their formative years, and the *influencers* that are affecting them today. It's probably a fair guess that a vast majority of people motor through life in a fog of how they see themselves, compounded by their impression or misperceptions, of how people actually see them.**

Henry Beckworth in *"Selling The Invisible"* wrote, "We think we are better than we are...Our illusions of superiority are so wide-spread that psychologists have come up with a name for it. They call it the Lake Wobegon Effect, after Garrison Keillor's famous radio show sign-off from his fictional hometown of Lake Wobegon where the women are strong, the men are good looking and the children are all above average..."

There are many other personalities we come across every day. There are the narcissists whose actions don't typically mirror their high opinions of themselves. You have the people who coast through their days acting miserable because their heads are so far up their rear ends they can't see the forest for the trees. They don't see in themselves the wonderful attributes that their family and friends can see so readily. They move through life conspicuously acting as if some grievous injury has befallen them that is too powerful to overcome. If they would only stop for a moment and take a deeper look in the mirror, they might discover that their ongoing consternation about life isn't warranted. Perhaps if they saw more of the world and the depths of the real issues facing the majority of mankind, they might relook their foolish "woe is me" personas.

Other groups of people we see are those who are always striving to act, or look, like someone else. People who are following a path through life they don't buy into...often because that's the pathway their parents *encouraged* upon them. **You can't do what someone else wants you to do.**

I'm perplexed with the incredible numbers of alcoholics and drug addicts that are walking this planet. The statistics and results are sad, dangerous and very costly to society. I'm no boy scout and I do realize that some people have had a stick taken to them their entire lives. I feel for these people, but there are others readily disposed to depression, dementia, and dependency on drugs or alcohol. This disposition leads to them to chronic mental, emotional or physical illnesses. They live life on a merry-go-round of failure in personal and career. How many times do they become an abuser of other people, or abused themselves?

As idealistic and simple as it may sound, I profess that **life is endless potential if you approach it with an open heart and a clear mind.** But it's not going to be wonderful and incredibly beautiful every day. The sun doesn't come out every day of the year. It has to rain sometimes and as such, life can also be excruciatingly frustrating and challenging. There is no planning or predicting which of your days will be happy, and which of your days you will wish you had stayed in bed.

I remember a Johnny Hart "B.C." comic strip from around twenty years ago. Thor, the emotionally-advanced caveman, climbs a steep mountain to visit a white-bearded guru perched high above the world. Finding the wise old man after a dangerous and exhausting trek, Thor meekly asks, "What is life?"

The ancient long-bearded caveman looks up and thoughtfully replies, "Life is the limitless perpetuality of timeless infinite eternity."

With a tear in his right eye, Thor tenderly muses aloud, "That's wonderful."

Without missing a beat, the white-haired elder hands Thor an employee time-card and directs, "Great. Punch me out on the way down, won't you?"

Realize that for the most part, you have 8-9 decades on this planet. How you go about attacking life during this "almost century" is up to you. As one of the most incredible motivational speakers I've heard, W. Mitchell says, **"It's not what happens to you. It's what you do about it."** You can go at life for all you are worth with your absolute best effort and try inexorably to make a difference. Conversely, you can play the ostrich and simply muddle your way through, one boring day after another. Unfortunately, it seems to me the majority of world falls into the second category for a whole array of social and economic reasons far beyond my comprehension.

Let's go back to the premise of this chapter.

>Do you truly know who you are?

>**Are you comfortable in your own skin?**

>Are you achieving the success you would like, and deserve, in your personal relationships and in your career?

>**Is the way that you perceive yourself, the reality of how others see you?**

>Are you constantly in and out of the diet craze?

>Do you drink a little more than you believe you should?

>Are there pills or substances hidden somewhere in your home you'd rather not have your family or friends know about?

>**Do you look in the mirror and like who's looking back at you?**

In order to properly answer these questions, a couple of considerations are mandatory. First, you must not be putting on different faces and personalities for different "crowds." You have to be the same person 100% of the time. Sure you can dial up the formality of your approach and delivery but **you don't change the fundamentals of what's inside you.** You can't be a certain personality on the job, and then someone completely different at home or with your friends. Dr. Jekyll and Mr. Hyde can't even survive in a novel. Oh yes, just because you see yourself a certain way, doesn't mean the world sees you the same way.

The second consideration is that **how you project yourself with your actions means more than how you profess yourself to be with words.** You need to understand if your actions support, or contradict, who you believe yourself to be. Let me take this personal to illustrate my premise.

I spent the first decade of my career trying to be someone else. I never felt quite as good as my peers because of my modest upbringing. My limited wardrobe of polyester-based clothes weren't as good as my co-workers and my oil-guzzling car wasn't as flashy their newer vehicles. My family didn't have a place up north to escape for the week-end. I never jetted off to the Riviera to stay with friends or relatives. My humble abode...was a humble abode. My summer jobs weren't working at Dad's firm or sailing in the Mediterranean. My summer jobs were toiling on farms picking vegetables or working in mercilessly-overheated manufacturing plants making products like tooth-picks and tongue depressors. I worked for minimum wage and was glad to get it. I knew what it meant to get dirt and grease under your nails and sawdust in your mouth. With this in my mindset, I felt the need to be someone else.

With university and my first job in the marketing industry, it immediately hit me that I didn't measure up to the grade (I'll elaborate on this later). Every day, I felt hobbled by my background. To compensate for this, I became a very formal business person and pursued an extreme

"Type A" approach to my job. Now, I 'm not saying that there's anything wrong with working like a dog, except that as the years flew by, I realized I wasn't really enjoying what I was doing. The motivation behind all of my efforts wasn't in the right place for longer-term happiness and stability. It was great for remuneration and titles, but when I was with my family or friends I was funnier, goofier and felt fulfilled. At work, the formality of my approach sucked the fun, creativity and life right out of me. My health suffered because of my dual approach and my stomach was always in knots. My inner peace was shot. The whole game just didn't sit well at all and I certainly wasn't the best person I could be, or wanted to be. I was allowing myself to be caught up in what I perceived was important in life, or rather what others surrounding me, felt was important in life. With each passing year, I lost track of what made me unique, and someone worth being around. I lost who I was in the place that counts the most--inside me.

Years ago, I completed an exercise that changed the way I looked at my life, what I wanted to be, and how I needed to act. Working through it, I realized that I didn't truly understand my underpinnings and why I felt the need to be these two different people: One "workplace-Howard" and "one non-workplace-Howard." This simple and complex exercise changed my entire life. I've actually re-done this exercise at different stages of my career over the last 20 years and every time I learn something new about myself. With the better understanding of "who I was, who I am and who I wanted to be," I learned how to accept my flat sides and foibles and simply be *me*. I discovered how to make my actions fit my belief system and desires. I removed the inconsistencies between my actions and my belief of who I really was, deep inside.

Finding comfort in your own skin requires an honesty that most people are unable to muster, even when it comes down to their own good. We all have self-defense mechanisms to protect ourselves from things we don't like. We project onto other people. We lie to ourselves and rationalize the world. We create biases and prejudices to separate ourselves. We make promises to ourselves and others that we have no intention of keeping. We take on personalities that are like roles in a movie. These are all falsehoods and aren't at all healthy. **Until you take a really good look in the mirror, knowing that it might crack, you'll never be the best person you are meant to be.**

Let's begin this process with three statements.

1. **How you see yourself is not necessarily how the world sees you at all.** Bets are that the two are highly disconnected.

2. **Factors that influenced and molded your character early in life are still affecting how you function, feel and interact with others today.**

3. **If you're <u>not</u> happy within your own skin, you can change if:**

   -you are prepared to face hard facts like: how you are perceived is a greater reality than how you see yourself;

   -you can honestly give up actions that make you comfortable no matter how insuperable this may seem; and,

   -you create and stick to game-plan every day going forward.

I've shared the 3 charts on the next few pages with approximately 100 people over my career. In cases where the people were able to be honest, their feedback to me has been consistently positive. Almost to a person, they have said that they learned something about themselves that they had not really understood before. They discovered disconnects with how others viewed them, versus how they viewed themselves. They all determined that they weren't necessarily acting appropriately for who they wanted to be. This discovery was the beginning of change for every one of them. **With self-awareness and honesty, you can begin to find an approach to be more comfortable with whom you are.** Then it's up to you to have the intestinal fortitude to pursue your plan. No one else is going to clarify your destiny for you no manner how many mentors or coaches you have, or shrinks you pay to see. Shakespeare wrote, "*It is not in the stars to hold our destiny but in ourselves.*" It's up to you. You're the driver of your life and the keeper of your own destiny.

Fill out these 3 charts as carefully and truthfully as you can. You'll need a number of people close to you to complete some of the sections. When you've finished your sections, throw them out and start again. I guarantee that you won't be honest with yourself the first time through. In part, because you aren't digging deeply enough into your memories, or facing what was/is the reality of the situation. **To kick you into the right mind set, start out by answering the following questions.**

Remember, this is all about you. *It's not test.* Your goal is to find out who you really are. With this beginning, you can then move onward to help yourself be more comfortable in your own skin. Try to add a comment to support your answer. Determine your own ranking of 1-10 with 1 meaning total disagreement and 10 meaning total agreement.

1.   I have a fulfilling relationship with a significant other. ___

Comment:

2.   I live a healthy lifestyle. ___

Comment:

3.   I am comfortable being alone. ___

Comment:

4.   I network well and know a lot of the "right" people. ___

Comment:

5.   I am a good athlete and physically fit. ___

Comment:

6.   I am comfortable with how smart I am. ___

Comment:

7.   My family brings outs my best. ___

Comment:

8. I am a great parent. ___

Comment:

9. I sleep well every night. ___

Comment:

10. I am optimistic about my career. ___

Comment:

11. My financial future looks safe and bright. ___

Comment:

12. I feel loved. ___

Comment:

13. I am happy with my appearance. ___

Comment:

14. I see the world as a wonderful place filled with opportunities. ___

Comment:

15. I like being around other people. ___

Comment:

16. I am relatively patient with others. ___

Comment:

17. I use my non-working time well. ___

Comment:

18. I feel spiritually at peace. ___

Comment:

19. I don't take life too seriously. ___

Comment:

20. I feel emotionally stable a lot of the time. ___

Comment:

21. Life is worth living to the fullest. ___

Comment:

22. I feel the company I work for more cares about me as much as I care about them. ___

Comment:

23. My significant other is understanding and accepting of who I am. ___

Comment:

24. I am rewarded well by my company for my hard work and contribution. ___

Comment:

25. I am surrounded by a great posse of friends. ___

Comment:

26. I have lots of personal time to spend on myself. ___

Comment:

27. The unceasing barrage of bad news in the media does not get me down. ___

Comment:

28. I am the best person I can be. ____

Comment:

Go back and review your answers and your comments. Please remember that this entire exercise is only for you so there's no need to pull any punches. **Write down the truth.** If you can't add a comment or substantiation to your ranking, then you need to re-think that specific ranking. Total up your answers for each of the 28 statements and then group them below on the scale from 1-10 (10 being totally agree).

Ranking   **Number (totaling 28)**

1-2   ___

3-4   ___

5-6   ___

7-8   ___

9-10   ___

What have you discovered about yourself through these questions? If you have been truthful to yourself you probably have mixed results. If your rankings all fall within the 9-10 range then God Bless You because you are one happy, fulfilled and highly successful person. I would propose that the rest of us mortals range from 5-10, and even that would vary on any given day.

How do you get your rankings higher and more consistent across the questions? How do you get up into the 7-10 range? You can't be your best living below this range. Not for long, anyway. Perhaps the next few pages can help. Look to the following 3 Charts and try to recreate them for yourself on separate pieces of paper. Fill in each block on each chart. This exercise is going to take time so please don't think you can breeze through it in the time it takes to watch a rerun of *Friends* or pick-up last night's score results on ESPN.com. This isn't a ten minute exercise but if you do it diligently, it can help bring incredible clarity to you. The Charts are entitled:

Chart A   **"Who am I today?"**

Chart B   **"Who was I at age 11?"**

Chart C   **"Who do I wish to be and how do I get there?"**

Have some fun with the following charts and learn about yourself.

A page from a CEO's Diary

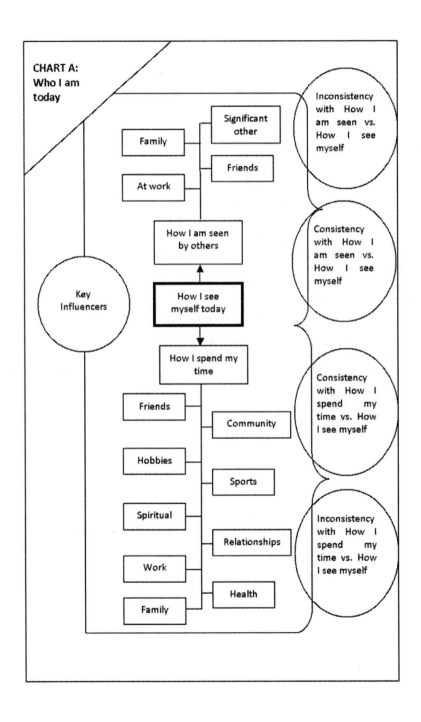

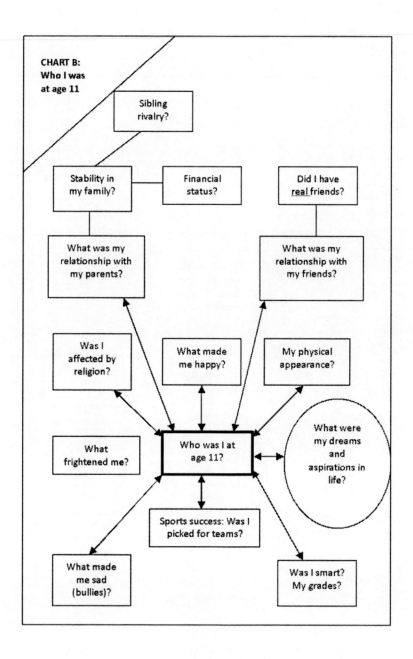

CHART B:
Who I was
at age 11

Sibling rivalry?

Stability in my family?

Financial status?

Did I have <u>real</u> friends?

What was my relationship with my parents?

What was my relationship with my friends?

Was I affected by religion?

What made me happy?

My physical appearance?

What frightened me?

Who was I at age 11?

What were my dreams and aspirations in life?

Sports success: Was I picked for teams?

What made me sad (bullies)?

Was I smart? My grades?

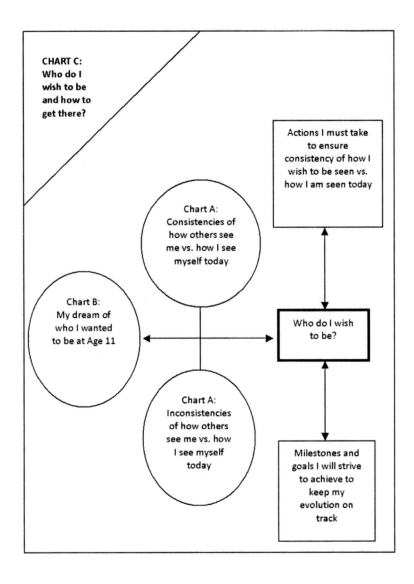

CHART C:
Who do I
wish to be
and how to
get there?

Actions I must take
to ensure
consistency of how I
wish to be seen vs.
how I am seen today

Chart A:
Consistencies of
how others see
me vs. how I see
myself today

Chart B:
My dream of
who I wanted
to be at Age 11

Who do I wish
to be?

Chart A:
Inconsistencies
of how others
see me vs. how
I see myself
today

Milestones and
goals I will strive
to achieve to
keep my
evolution on
track

Completing and understanding the charts: Chart A:

Who you are is not necessarily how you see yourself in the centre box. There are key influencers surrounding the centre box that affect your whole life. How do these influencers, both positive and negative, affect how you see yourself today? Do you control these influencers, or do they control you? If you don't like how you are being affected, then what can you do to make some changes? Understand how you are influenced by:

-your health

-your appearance

-your age, sex, ethnicity

-your religion

-your family, friends, boss and co-workers

-your job

-your financial situation and future prospects

-your home-life

Carry this to the next level and move to the bottom right half of the chart (below the centre box). How, and with whom, are you spending your time? Break out 100 hours and place percentages against each of:

<u>%</u>

-friends __

-community __

-hobbies __

-sports __

-spiritual __

-relationships __

-work/job __

-health __

-family __

I can imagine that your biggest percent is work-related and your lowest percents are likely spiritual and community. That's how my numbers tend to fall out. Am I right?

Now look back the 2 circles immediately to the right of this section. Identify the consistencies and inconsistencies in how you actually spend your time versus how you should be spending your time based on the centre box of **"How you see yourself."**

Move to the top half of the chart and begin to fill in **"How I am seen by others."** How would others describe you based on your interaction, and attitude towards them? You realize they judge you on your actions...not just your words?

Look to the 2 circles immediately to the right of this section. Identify in writing the consistencies and inconsistencies in **"How others see you" versus "How you see yourself."**

Fill in what you have learned from Chart A:

_____
_____
_____
_____
_____
_____

Completing and understanding the Charts: Chart B

This is an extremely critical exercise to complete and requires you to think back very carefully to your youth. This is the most difficult of the three charts. You need to consider every single box on the page before you can reframe and reconstruct, **"Who I was at age 11."** At that age, we were pre-puberty and caught between thinking and acting like a kid, and wanting to be treated like an adult. It was an incredibly awkward state but it was a time of hope and "child-like" perspectives on life. We had not been jaded by the world when we were eleven. We were just beginning to see life.

After you address every box, including the centre box, I would like you to complete the circle on the right of the page. "What were your dreams and aspirations?" I often ask this question to people and about 30% of the time, the responses are very close reflecting what the responder is doing as an adult. These people appear happy and content. The remaining 70% of the respondents smile warmly about their memories and dreams, and then instantaneously offer up excuses for not having fulfilled those dreams. These are the people who more that often are doing exactly the opposite of what they felt was possible when they were eleven. They are not living their inner dreams.

When you complete Chart B, please don't ignore the sections including:

>what frightened me?

>what made me sad?

>what made me happy?

Completing and understanding the charts: Chart C

This is the build chart of the three. If you've sincerely completed Charts A and B, then this will fall easily into place. Bring forward your dreams and aspirations from Chart B and then cross-reference from Chart A, the consistencies and inconsistencies of how others see you versus how you see yourself. Boy that was hard to get out!

How does it look? Are there serious contradictions? As I said earlier, it tends to be a 30/70 game. 30% of the time, people are pretty close to doing what's in their heart...what they thought about when they were younger. They surround themselves with influencers that help them achieve their goals. They dedicate their time accordingly to making it work for them. They spend time with people they should, doing things in life that support who they believe they are. The remaining **70% of the people are at odds with themselves, with their family/friends and how they are spending their time. They live in a contradiction of actions and beliefs.**

Move to the box on the right of Chart C. Having considered everything to this point, you need to take a step away from the table. **"Who do you wish to be?"** How different is this from Chart A's "How I see myself today?" Don't be over-whelmed if there are major gaps. This is the first step only.

You now have tackled the exercise of the 3 Charts. What actions must you take to help you become the person you wish to be? What must you do to ensure consistency in how you wish to be seen versus "How people see you today?" Write down five actions, no matter how difficult or insurmountable they seem to be.

1. _____
   _____
   _____
   ___

2. _____
   _____
   _____
   ___

3. _____
   _____
   _____
   ___

4. _____
   _____
   _____
   ___

5. _____
   _____
   _____
   ___

This was probably a very difficult exercise to work through. The actions you have just written down will evolve with time and as you make changes to your life. **This is not a one-time exercise and it really requires you to have an open mind, and to enlist the help of those close to you.**

In order to avoid falling back into bad habits and actions that aren't healthy for you, write down a number of milestones which you will use as goal-posts to judge your progress.

1._____

2._____

3. _____

Remember, **your life is not a dress-rehearsal**. It you fall into the 70% camp of not doing in life what you feel in your heart you should be doing, then it's time to make a change. You can build your own plan, set your own course, engage some help, and just do it. You can do this if you set your heart to it and don't relent.

Desmond Tutu wrote, *"You are a very special person—become what you are."*

Chapter 1 Key:

The probability of you achieving greater success in your career, relationships and in life increases exponentially with how well you: know yourself; like and admire yourself; and, display consistency between your actions and who you are inside.

Chapter 2

"Life is either a great adventure or nothing…"

-Helen Keller

Your life is much more than your job, money, home, family and friends. It's more than going to the gym or out to see a movie or hit a club. Life has to be more than a great holiday each year and fun week-ends. **There is so much more to experience and the world is bursting over with challenges and adventures just waiting for someone to come along and tackle them.**

Let me tell you about a really cool adventure I tackled a couple of years ago. I ran a marathon. Now this is not something for everyone. I simply want to share one story to serve as an example of what happens to you when you go after a challenge you aren't certain you can overcome and beat.

Years ago, I completed my first marathon in 1970 at the tender age of fourteen. I carefully chose the word "completed." I had not prepared in the absolute least so I can't claim that I "ran" it…even if part of the race I did run. I hadn't the foggiest idea of what was in store for me and totally ignored my parents' sound advice to perhaps "give this a second thought." I was fourteen and knew more than they did! Didn't we all at fourteen?

"What's the problem with completing a marathon?" I asked incredulously, as if both of my parents were complete morons. "I've got nothing better to do on Saturday, and I'm bored. What's the big deal?"

The Owen Sound Marathon was in fact a 29 mile run/walk for charity sponsored by the YMCA. This marathon was 29 miles rather than the *sanctioned* distance of 26.2 miles because the organizers who mapped out the route, couldn't find a way of cutting out 2.8 miles. So they left it at 29 miles and hoped for the best. Along with two hundred others, I showed up in the parking lot of a local mall. It was 7:00 am and I was bone-tired from having gotten to bed late the night before. The organizers welcomed everyone, told us to line up, and a starter's pistol was fired. It was a really hot morning and within ten minutes I had worked up quite a sweat. I had forgotten to bring a hat, or suntan lotion. I had a sandwich for lunch and a bottle of Coke. I remember that I was wearing a pair of limp running shoes (this was before my episode with my God- forsaken Adidas which I'll tell you about in a later chapter). My dad drove around the route four times during the day to ask if I wanted to "call it a day."

"Never," I replied steadfastly, firming my resolve and pushing forward.

At mile 20, I began battling the early stages of sunstroke along with a golf-ball-sized blister forming on my left knee. Being true to a persistent Breen, I wouldn't quit. The race started officially at 8:00 am and I ran across that damned finish line at 3:45 pm. I finished just shy of 7 hrs 45 minutes and it had been 6 hrs and 45 minutes of unbearable hell. After crossing the finish line at City Hall, I stumbled off to my home with feet of clay and a mind of mush. It was as if I had just completed an entire decathlon in one afternoon. I sat frozen like a dime-store mannequin for hours... my entire well-being and spirit decimated. I felt dead.

"I'll never to that again," I promised myself and my family with certitude. "I should have listened." That night and for the next day I was delirious with sun-stroke. I had a migraine that would have sunk the Titanic. I couldn't get enough water inside me without throwing it back up. It took me a week to come back to life.

"Never again," I repeated to myself, amazed at my stupidity.

I can honestly report that heart-felt promise endured for almost four decades.

Then my promise hit the skids. Perhaps the true memories of the aftermath waned with the passage of time. Perhaps in my older immaturity I still knew better than others who questioned my sanity. You see, I turned fifty years-old and the proverbial question entered my mind about my longevity: *Do you realize you are closer to the end than the beginning?* What a disgusting and morbid thought. With my rapidly approaching mortality staring me down like a deer caught in the headlights, I sat back and thought of the kinds of adventures I could pursue that would help spark me, keep me healthy, and show the world that turning fifty really wasn't that much of a big deal.

So, thirty-six years after I made that promise about *never running another marathon*, I began training for my second marathon adventure. This "officially sanctioned" marathon was run in Toronto and was accurately measured to 26.2 miles, unlike the 29 miler that had almost killed me. I prepped, cross-trained, dieted and pushed myself to the limit for over eighteen months. I worked my way up to the full 26.2 miles by getting back into shape for a 5K YMCA corporate run. I then graduated to the 10K Terry Fox Run, which led to the Ottawa Half-Marathon. I kept pushing the training harder and with the drastic loss of weight and arrival of runner's legs, I knew that the adventure was truly underway. Do you know that I was up to 40-45 miles per week? I even managed to get that "gaunt" long distance runner look. You know the look: tanned faced, highly exaggerated cheek bones, and what appears to be a totally undernourished physique. My biceps and triceps become a thing of the past and my butt disappeared. Ah, I looked great. Quelle adventure! I had to have the waist of every pair of pants taken in over 3 inches. I had to buy new belts and bathing suits. I was a sleek, mean running machine.

As time passed, the thrill of the adventure took on a different meaning as my body and spirit were entering the realms of exhaustion. In the latter stages of training, the preparation for the marathon took unwavering dedication, intense focus and concentration. My persistence was all that kept me going. It was intriguing but I discovered that after I shared my training stories with my friends and co-workers, a few starting actually picking up the "running bug," and started running 5K and 10K races. While my training was underway, I met a whole new group of people and athletes that I would otherwise never have come across. People of like-minded habits and adventures are drawn to each other. The commonality of the goal and training is something you want to share.

I also discovered that running a marathon includes a real understanding of nutrition and eating habits. I had to learn all about those and the importance of carbohydrates. Running also requires a different kind of commitment...one from your significant other and your children.

The training is painfully exhausting and it involves a commitment from the whole family. Running 40-50 miles every week physically involves a lot of time which means missing doing things with your family. Having special meals prepared pre-race that perhaps they don't like. I also discovered I could only deliver my mileage by getting up incredibly early each morning. So every Sunday, I religiously awoke at 5:00 am to have my pre-run meal. I would start my run at 7:00 am, and be home by 11:00 am. This took me away from home and our ritual Sunday morning walk with the dog. I did schedule to spend the rest of every Sunday with my kids. Admittedly, I was bone-stiff with exhausted and tender muscles. I appreciated that my family understood my adventure and helped me through it. This is a key point to picking, and pursuing your adventure. You need to solicit the support of those around you.

Life continues on while you are tackling your adventure. *Time stands still for no man*. Wherever I travelled on business or on vacation, I ran. I saw more of the world running than I ever did before. Always heeding safety, I would run the local areas at 6:00 am before the city awoke and the roads filled with cars. There is nothing like running the coastline of a Greek island as the sun is coming up over the Mediterranean, and smelling the salt air as it hits your face. It's absolutely intoxicating. Running through Rome, New York, Athens, Chicago, San Francisco shows you sides of the cities you would likely miss on a business trip, or vacation.

By the way, another positive off-shoot of being so focused on one sport or activity is that the contribution and thinking I brought to my company increased three-fold. My mind was focused and clear. The running afforded me time to think about the company, my family, my future and my health. Co-incidentally, it also allowed me to *not think* about the company, my family, my future and my health. It allowed me to just "be."

If you out there reading this are a runner then you know exactly what I'm talking about. For those of you who have thought about taking up running whether for health, sport or excitement, I can only tell you that it was, and is one of the best things I've ever done in my life.

So how did my adventure all turn out? Let me tell you. The weather that Sunday morning was perfect with a cool crisp air, clear blue skies and a slight breeze off Lake Ontario. A crowd over ten thousand filled the streets around the starting line and my heart had never pounded so hard in my entire life. Everyone was nervous and anticipating the best. I was shivering with the freshness of the morning air...and my nervousness. My wife, children and sister would be awaiting me at the finish line in four hours. I had told everyone I knew about this marathon. Friends would be following along by checking out my part-times on the marathon's web-site. I was as anxious as could be. The starter's pistol fired and after inching my way up to the official starting line, I was off. Lord knows why but I screamed out some unintelligible cry, and laughed. I felt such exhilaration that I had never felt before. Once you begin running, you are bumped and must avoid being tripped, or tripping someone else. It takes about fifteen minutes for your heart to settle down, your wind to come in and your groove and pace to be established. The miles flew under my Asics and I was on track for a beautiful sub-4 hour finish. At the 3 hour mark I was right on time and feeling great. "What a wonderful adventure," I thought to myself, as I waved at friends along the course. Any memories from my first marathon had long escaped me as I approached the home-stretch. And then very unexpectedly, I got hit with a charley-horse in my left thigh. I had just pulled in behind a really strong runner when it happened. We were rounding a slight bend when my left leg cramped up, and I was forced to pull over and stretch. I had only 3.2 miles to go and I could barely stand up straight. My leg felt like a razor-sharp machete was sticking through it. Cursing at the pain and unfairness of the whole mishap, I hit the pavement again. I determined that come "hell or high water" I would not stop. I hadn't trained for 18 months to quit on the side of the road. I struggled to prove to myself just what I was made of. No matter what I do in the rest of my life, I will always remember the pain of that last thirty minutes and then seeing my family standing by the finish line. Their faces and cheers filled my heart and I straightened up and ran my guts out to the tape. I didn't quite make my 4 hour target but I had tackled a great adventure and come out alive to talk about it.

I continued with my training and after running a number of other races, I fell and buggered up my left knee. For the record, I was not running at the time. I ripped my left meniscus which is a pancake-shaped cushion inside your knee joint. I had to stop further training and have an operation to repair it. I was scheduled for arthroscopic surgery to repair the ripped meniscus in my left knee. During my recovery from the surgery, I had the pleasure of talking with John Stanton, the founder of The Running Room. I've had the pleasure of meeting John on several occasions. He is one of these exceptionally driven, highly inspirational people who make you feel wonderful about yourself every time you see him. He lives for adventures. John is a well-known runner and author of numerous running and motivational books. During our conversation, John looked at me and said, *"Howard, you'll be back up running before you know it and all this will be a memory to help drive you further down the road. Keep your mind on your goal and don't let anything divert your from it."* He was right. It's not the easiest of adventures to pursue but it you are going to pursue an adventure, why pick an easy one? I've begun my training again.

Think on this a moment. What are you doing to physically and emotionally push yourself to the limit? **What have you dreamed about doing that you just haven't gotten around to?** This chapter is not about running a marathon. I've only used that as an example of setting out to do something that will push you to your limit. What is an adventure that you would love to pursue? It is never too late. All you have to do is make up your mind and then just do it. Read this list I pulled together for you.

1.   Whitewater rafting on the Colorado

2.   Hiking Machu Pichu in Peru

3.   Motorcycling tours through Spain and Portugal

4.   Flying in an F-16 or MIG-29

5.   Speed racing in high performance cars

6.   Climbing Mt. Kilimanjaro

7.   Cycling across Canada and the USA

8.   Sailing in the Caribbean or Mediterranean

9.   Running a marathon

10. Walking along the Great Wall of China

11. Kayaking in Costa Rica, Canada or Iceland

12. Skydiving Mt. Everest

13. Skiing or snowboarding in Chile

14. Safari in Kenya or Egypt

15. Trekking across Nepal

Now from this list, or other ideas you've had, **write down five adventures that you would love to pursue and accomplish over the next ten years.** Do not consider cost, location or work conflicts. Once you determine your goal, then you will figure out the logistics. Five adventures would be:

1._____

2._____

3. _____

4. _____

5. _____

Life is 24 hour a day and seven days a week...not just on Saturdays and Sundays. It's not "letting go" while you are on your vacations. With each passing year, you'll find time speeding up. With each passing decade, you'll wonder where time has gone. If you have children, your life becomes measured by their height, and their progress. That can't be all there is to it. **Grabbing at life means reaching out and tackling something new and amazing.** Don't let work days be only work days. Use your lunches. Go for a walk or to a museum. Every day get outside and look at the sky. Getting to each adventure will be as rewarding as completing them. Mark Twain said, *"Plan for the future because that is where you are going to spend the rest of your life."*

Now go back to each of the five adventures you wrote above. Investigate them on the Internet. Talk to friends who may have knowledge and experience that they can share with you. **Don't let dreams disappear until you're too old to do them.** Set out a plan that gives you a new adventure every two years. In ten years, imagine what you will have accomplished. Make the plan achievable but far-reaching so you have to prepare yourself mentally, emotionally and physically. Engage your family in your planning.

I can imagine that some of you are overwhelmed by the idea of climbing a mountain, or tackling a marathon. Don't let this stop you from having other kinds of adventures. We each have different tolerance and risk levels. There are so many things for you to take on. Consider adventure-weekends with outings that could include paintballing, go-karting, caving, rock-wall climbing, snorkeling/scuba diving, laser tag, ultimate Frisbee or joining a soccer or volleyball league. Seek out a tackle or a challenge that's right for you. **Don't let your days pass you by waiting for something to happen.** You can never fully know what's coming your way no matter how hard you try to anticipate life. *"God made the world round so we couldn't see too far down the road,"* wrote Isak Dineson.

Chapter 2 Key:

Life is as wonderful as you make it. Don't just live for week-ends or holidays. Make every day count. Set out to achieve adventures that stretch and challenge you to the limit.

Chapter 3

"Everyone is born a genius, but the process of living de-geniuses them..."

-R. Buckminster Fuller

Can you remember being eleven? Years ago, I was having dinner with one of my favorite clients of all time. Mr. Malcolm Seath was the President of Whitehall Robins Canada, and along with a very solid scientific mind, he had the most incredible way of looking at life. Over dinner with our wives, he turned to me and asked, *"Howard, what were you like when you were eleven or twelve?"*

"That's an unusual question Malcolm," I replied cautiously. He waited a moment until I shared with the table what things I was up to at that early age. I smiled as I spoke about the aspirations I had when I was eleven. I remembered vividly that I wanted to fly in airplanes and ride trains...two things I had yet to do. I told him that at eleven I was a shrimp and all I wanted was to be picked first for some game. Perhaps one day to be the captain of a team. I also loved being with my family and had the kind of household, parents and siblings that you rushed home to be with. Malcolm smiled and shared the thinking behind his question. His perspective was that **you should be doing today what you thought you should be doing when you were eleven.** If you were, you would likely be a very happy person. If you weren't, you were not being true to what was in the foundation of your formative years. You'd likely find yourself an unhappy person.

How wise Malcolm's question was that night. I've thought a lot about that question over the years. Three years after that dinner, I was working out of Chicago in a North American role that required me to fly numerous times each week. I was in hotels 25% of my working time. My family lived on the north shore of the city in Winnetka, and

I commuted daily by train into downtown Chicago. I was the CEO of numerous operations around the continent, and was regularly being selected for "special teams." Most of the time, I led those teams...like a Captain. My home life was idyllic. I was as happy as a clam. I was reminded of our dinner with the Seaths, and I recalled Malcolm's sage counsel. I was living the life I had imagined when I was eleven.

When we are children, the world is still a vast and promising thought. The idea of its size and opportunities opens and fills our minds and imaginations. We picture different places around the world based on pictures and movies, and a vision of those images takes root. In our play time we travel the world on great adventures. I know I went to the Great Wall of China as Genghis Khan. As I kid, I found myself in England battling William the Conqueror and the next day at the Alamo fighting with Davy Crockett. I was forever seeking the source of the Nile with Sir Richard Burton or aboard Jules Verne's Nautilus with Captain Nemo. Along the way, I also discovered the cure for cancer and hit a home run in Game 7 of the World Series against the Yankees. Playing along-side Gordie Howe and Jean Beliveau, I scored more game winning goals than any player in the NHL. I stood on Everest with Sir Edmund. **As children, our minds take us to places our eyes might never see.**

It's with the passage of time, and the gaining of more birthdays that these imaginings either become a positive reality, or erode with the relentless piling on of accountabilities, jobs, relationships and financial pressures. As we get physically larger, many people become smaller in spirit and imagination. **Imagination is hardly a match for the brutality of too much reality**.

Take a moment and pick up a pen. Who were you at eleven? What were your dreams and aspirations? Did you have any idea of what activities you found really cool or exciting? Now, with the same pen, write down if you are fulfilling any part of those dreams? I hope you are. I ask this question to people regularly and I don't often get an affirmative answer. There is truth in each of our own personal histories. The trick is not having that truth muddled with the passage of time.

<u>**At eleven, I wanted to:**</u>   <u>**Fulfilling it today?**</u>

1. _____   _____

2. _____   _____

3. _____   _____

4. _____   _____

5. _____   _____

George Bernard Shaw wrote that, *"Imagination is the beginning of creation. You imagine what you desire, you will what you imagine and at last you create what you will."* How is it that some people continue to foster their imagination throughout their whole lives? I believe it's because deep inside, they've learned the secret of protecting their "child-like" spirit which is the catalyst for a wonderful and furtive imagination. With this imagination comes the willpower to make it real. How do we protect that "child-like" spirit that is in each of us when we are born? We start out in life with vivid imaginations that see animals in clouds forms and uncover fun in the mundane. Did your bright world that was filled with optimism get clouded over? You know what I mean. The years do have an effect on us all. Time can erode spirit the same way that wind will take the best topsoil off a farmer's field. How does that farmer protect his field? First, he recognizes the potential threat. Second, his experience tells him the threat is not going to go away, and must be dealt with. Third, he plants trees and builds fences around the perimeter of his farm. Now as each day and night passes, he intently watches the weather, and instigates systems of irrigation to address the dryness, and retard the erosion of his topsoil.

Your spirit and your soul are like that farmer's field. Most people allow time to come at them like a lightning storm while they are standing outside in a suit of metal armor flying a kite. They get bashed in year after year until their spirit is sucked dry. Cynicism and pessimism replace that spirit of youth and it does its best to extinguish curiosity, compassion and hope. Mark Twain wrote, *"There is nothing sadder than a young pessimist."*

Getting older does not have to mean looking at the glass half empty. It doesn't have to make you look at life with dark glasses on. Remember the positives as you make your way through the day. If the news of the day is depressing then don't read it so you can become over-wrought. Turn off the radio. It's okay to play ostrich sometimes. That news will keep coming at you as sure as CNN repeats the same stories

40 times each day. In fact, *"turn off the television,"* Al Gore wrote in his best-selling book, *"The Assault on Reason."* The Nobel Prize winner and former Vice President also wrote,

"I'm not saying television viewers are like hypnotized chickens... experience tells me that extended television watching can be mind-numbing."

Surround yourself with people who are positive. Find excuses to spend more time with your kids, and younger nieces and nephews. Study their approach to life and learn from it. Re-invigorate your batteries to help you face each day, month and year with a positive and curious outlook on life. Don't let your attitude go to the *dark side*. *"Be curious, not judgmental,"* wrote Walt Whitman.

Extend your mental reach into new and exciting areas. With every person with whom you interact, immediately ask what they are reading: which books, magazines or blogs. Write down their answer, and then invest some time seeing why those materials caught their eye.

The next time you plan a vacation do something totally out of the ordinary. As I wrote in the previous chapter on **life is an adventure,** don't do the customary routine vacation. Plan a trip that will require you to study and learn in preparation. Don't just go and sit on a beach with a tiny pink umbrella adorning your colorful drink. Make yourself more interesting by instigating your curiosity and imagination to be catalysts for learning and broadening your horizons.

Write down 3 vacation destinations you'd love to go to:

1. _____

2. _____

3. _____

Is there an insurmountable reason why you can't get to two of these destinations in the next five years? If you only had five years to live...wouldn't you find a way to make this work for you?

Take more interesting trips and you'll find more people will want you around. Your job will pick up. Your imagination will be rejuvenated and ideas will come to you like never before. If you can muster a little gumption and willpower you can bring those ideas to life. You will be a much better person to your mate. You'll also discover that as the wind approaches your field, your soil will remain grounded...as will you and your "child-like" spirit.

Think back to being eleven. What did you know then...that you don't know now?

Chapter 3 Key:

Don't let life suck the child out of you. Keep your curiosity and imagination firing on all cylinders.

Chapter 4

"Take your partners with you..."

-Golda Meir 1977

Who are your "life guides?" Throughout my life, older people in more senior positions have helped guide me through my career. Without their wisdom, caring and guidance I would never have become a CEO. Of this statement, I have no doubt. As you begin your career you need to set out a number of potential scenarios just as you did in selecting your courses at university or college. Few people starting out can map out exactly what they want to be doing in life. In fact, I wasn't really sure what I wanted to be doing in life until my late twenties. Even now, I encounter a large number of individuals, beyond their twenties, who still haven't "discovered themselves" and what they should be doing in life. So it's vital you take the time to map out a series of potential avenues for your life. These should be "springboards" you would find both appealing and financially viable.

Recognize that **as time passes, you are going to face forks in the road**. This is perfectly natural for us all and I hope you must make lots of decisions on which forks to pursue. If you aren't meeting forks in the road you are either an extremely lucky person who's perfectly happy and on track with their life, or you are like the rest of the world still searching for the "next" thing. I imagine most of us will be facing forks. This is where it becomes really difficult on you. You will likely not have the basis of true experience and wisdom to know which road to follow. Your mate, friends and family can be called on for their input, but their advice may not be grounded in rich experience. Their advice may be jaded by ulterior motives. Be especially careful not to fall into the trap of doing what your parents want. Their intentions may be good but also tainted in having you pursue roads that perhaps they wished they had pursued themselves...but did not.

Who then can you turn to for unbiased honest counsel? CEOs have a Board of Directors. Usually, independent business leaders who come together quarterly to help advise the CEO on business issues, while ensuring his/her actions are within the agreed-to limits of corporate governance. The Board members are carefully selected and often remunerated for their input. Not all of us are CEOs with a Board of Directors. That does not mean that we can't set up a council of more senior, and experienced people to help us formulate our thinking as life progresses.

I term these people my "life guides." For expediency of typing and reading, allow me to short-form these as **LGs**. From the time I graduated university, I realized I needed help and advice from non-family members. I didn't rush out to "solicit" people to become my LGs. I simply watched people with whom I worked: People in the business world who deserved admiration. Senior leaders whose approach to business I wished to emulate. One by one, I added these people to my list of LGs. I was fortunate to belong to the Young Presidents' Organization (YPO) where it was possible to spend good rich time interacting with Presidents in various stages of their careers. Some had made it big while others had lost it big. Some had made fortunes, lost them and were back to making them again. Within YPO, each member was included in a "forum" of 8-10 other YPO'ers. The forum served as a highly confidential board of directors for each of the members. It was incredible for me as a *junior* President and I was blessed with the most incredibly insightful and caring forum imaginable.

Most of you reading this book are not Presidents. You don't have access to an organization like the YPO, or the forums that come along with it. As such, you need to seriously bring to your table, senior leaders who can help un-clutter your mind, clarify options facing you, and help you to see various courses of action that are in your best interest to investigate. Your **LGs are mentors whose words you will heed and whose actions you will watch and incorporate into your style.** I'm not telling you to become a mindless clone. I'm suggesting that you try to emulate the best of what you see these successful people achieving.

Like any Board of Directors, people will fulfill the role of LG for you and then one of you will move on. It's vital you not overstay your welcome with your LGs. If you are wise, you won't keep your LGs with you for a long time. As you get older, you will find that what might have been a one-way street becomes a two-way street with you being the advice giver. With time, these mentors will have watched you grow and evolve. They will have witnessed you succeeding and failing. This will allow their wisdom to play an even stronger role for you moving forward. Similarly, with time, you will have learned: a) if you have selected wisely in choosing your mentors; and, b) how successfully their lives and careers have continued to unfold.

I have been extremely fortunate to have been counseled and nurtured by incredible mentors. I've chosen my LGs, or rather in some cases, have been chosen by my LGs at critical junctions in my career. A few have known me from the time I only owned two polyester suits and was earning $14,000.00 per year. They've watched me succeed and stumble, and have stuck by me throughout the years. Other mentors have joined my journey along the way. In both cases, I have benefitted from the generosity of these wonderful people and the wisdom they have imparted to me.

Don't rush to find mentors and for goodness sake never ask someone to be your mentor. That's just bad form. I've had complete strangers ask me to be their mentor which is not something I welcomed at all. When you've determined a potential LG, you must begin the relationship slowly and let it unfold in the right manner. You will see if the person is willing to get to know you and potentially take you under their wing. Just because you've decided someone could be your mentor doesn't mean that they will accept the role.

Looking back, I will readily admit that when I heeded the sound advice and counsel of my mentors, prosperity and success followed. **The three times in my life that I ignored the collective advice of my LGs I stumbled and failed miserably.** Brick walls and setbacks followed. It took considerable time and many sleepless nights to get back on track.

Allow me to share an example of one of my LGs. I normally don't discuss my mentors, who they are, or any advice they've ever given me. That should be held in complete confidence. This example is treated with extreme reverence.

Mr. Gordon Barnes and I met over 15 years ago, while I was vacationing with my family in Marco Island, Florida. Gordon and Joan

Barnes owned a condo where my mother-in-law was renting each winter. A very successful business man, Gordon and his wife had two grown children and a number of lovely grandchildren. His career was in the world of banking and Gordon seemed to have an incredible grasp on balancing work and family. Each year, we visited with the Barnes at spring break. Ironically, we didn't communicate throughout the remained eleven months of the year. As spring break and the upcoming escape to Marco approached, I could hardly wait to see the Barnes, and talk with Gordon. His opinions were well-founded and his wisdom was worth its weight in gold. He listened attentively to everything I had to say and would interject with very insightful questions at key points. He never foisted his opinion(s) on me but would share his experience. I learned to gobble up that experience and thank God I did. Here are four things Gordon helped me to see at various stages of my career.

1. You can't get rich earning a salary and a bonus when the latter comes at the "whim" of your seniors. You must seek out jobs in companies that are either destined to go public or be bought by a larger corporation. You must be able to take advantage of the vesting of stock options and the relative tax breaks that come with capital gains. Carefully research companies and secure positions accordingly. Once the company has gone public and you've made your "financial hit" there is no need to stay longer and simply become a salaried employee losing half your earnings to taxation. If you are in a public company, you must be compensated accordingly with stock and options that will allow proper growth to make your vesting and time investment worthwhile.

2. Life exists beyond Canada. Get out and see the world and look for an international posting. With each posting, your skill sets, marketability and maturity will advance dramatically. Your family's cohesiveness will increase ten-fold with a loving interdependence resulting.

3. Plan your investments to minimize risk. This is a long-term game, not a sprint to the finish. Investing is like dieting. The faster you try to get a quick payback, the faster you will lose your money. Dieting is a slow methodical process. Lose pounds quickly and gain them back quickly. *Slow and steady investing wins the race.*

I heeded Gordon's advice throughout my career, and of all my mentors, he had a penchant for helping to guide my life with extreme care and incontrovertible advice. His thinking was always unselfish and true. Gordon Barnes died in 2002, the same year I lost my Mother. It was an inexplicable and totally uncalled-for one-two combination that knocked me to the mat for an eight count. I miss having him in my life and can only hope that someone out there learns as much from me as I did from Gordon Barnes.

Your LGs are mentors who are vital to your future. Seek them carefully and try to bring diversity of experience and culture to your personal Board. Don't waste your counselors' time and don't expect that they will have all the answers. They don't necessarily have to even know each other and the odds are that you will never meet with more than one at a time. You must never breach the confidentiality of your conversations.

With the passage of time you may find yourself becoming a life guide or mentor to a younger person. Take this role seriously and don't be giving "off the cuff" advice. Your counsel will carry a great deal of weight and can have serious consequences on the successes or failures of another person.

Chapter 4 Key:

We all need help and guidance throughout our lives. Choose people with wisdom and experience to be your "life guides." Don't go it alone.

Chapter 5

"Don't be afraid to see what you see…"

-Ronald Reagan

Through what filters do you see the world? I learned a valuable lesson early in life that I remind myself of on a regular basis. Do you have a filter in your head that: a) you employ before you speak; and, b) that you call upon to help frame your thinking on a daily basis?

First, let's discuss the verbal filter. How many of your family members, friends and co-workers speak without thinking? Do you? It shocks me at how many people think that they can blurt out anything, gauge the reaction, and then apologize if they have spoken out of turn. You have those people in your life, right? Don't be one of them. Once words pass your lips they are out there for good. Same applies to anything you write or e-mail. Words spoken, or written are permanent. Even a quick and sincere apology for hurtful, or thoughtless words will only dull the damage you inflicted but it will not *remove* it. The severe damage caused to another's feelings remains long after you apologize. It can mar a relationship forever, just like an unexpected slap across the face. How your words can irreparably damage someone is almost incomprehensible…but true. **Before you speak, hesitate and think about the consequences of your words.** Are you interacting with respect? Are you being clear in what you are meaning to say? Are you responding on an even keel , or with emotions uncontrolled? Words can cut *like a knife*. Sometimes you want that knife brought out…but only after considered thought and a firm decision to do so. Set a filter in your mind that helps you hesitate for 5 seconds before you open your trap.

A couple of years ago, I saw former President Bill Clinton address an audience in New York. What an incredible mind and inspirational orator. He spoke of the filters through which he interprets events around the world. **Clinton clarified that one of his filters, in looking at all new global events, is "how these events would fit within the global community."** Another blinding glimpse of the obvious for me, but I realized that I hadn't really formulated my own thinking about filters and how to assimilate world events. I judge people and ideas very distinctly. After 50+ years on the planet, how I look at events unfolding around the world is very different than I did in my youth. It's the same for you. After the Clinton speech, I analyzed my filters to ensure that they were the kind of filters that were acceptable to me. As I write this, it sounds like a foolish exercise. But it wasn't. We all have prejudices inside us whether we want to admit it or not. **We have pre-conceived notions about others that can negatively hamper our thoughts, interactions and decisions**. I realized that my filters had a very strong Canadian component to them. As my business career entered its 4th decade, my filters were becoming too limited, and focused on the monetary aspect of life. I realized that I needed to think differently about the world. Disasters like the Tsunami in December, 2006 or Hurricane Katrina in 2007 demand a more global viewpoint and interpretation.

Given all of this, I changed my filters and I'm certain that with maturity and time, they will change again. Now, I try to take in world events with a mindset that *I can help*, not that "they really have nothing to do with me." I believe that *I can make a difference*. I can donate money. I can invest my time in charitable causes that make a difference. **I don't have to be a bystander**.

When I refined and cleaned out my filters, my entire persona changed. I no longer take a back seat and observe from a safe distance. I don't put down the newspaper and move on to the next thing on my plate. I have now taken a more active role by engaging in my community. My filters have helped me broaden my whole personality. What filters are you seeing the world through? How do you gather news of global events? Be en garde against depending solely on your television news which Dan Rather was quoted as having been, *"dumbed down and tarted up."* Solicit your news from a variety of news programs and web-sites. Are your current filters holding you back from actually being the best person you can be? Are they protecting and shielding you from being sucked dry by all the foolishness that the world can throw at you?

Chapter 5 Key:

We are over-exposed to much nastiness in the world on a daily basis. It can take the wind out of your sails. Utilize mental filters through which you see, and interact with, the world. Ensure your filters help you understand how you fit within events occurring outside of your sphere of influence. Get off the side-lines and into the game. Use a mental filter to slow you down before you speak.

Chapter 6

"We can do anything we want if we stick to it long enough...

-Helen Keller

I am repeatedly asked what the one quality is that I possess that helped me to become a CEO. In particular, when this is posed to me by more junior employees, I turn around the question and ask them to answer it for me. I challenge them to pick 5 qualities from the list below that would have helped me get the corner office. I then ask them to select the *one* quality above all that made the difference. Scan this list and pull out what you believe to be the five most vital qualities leading to success.

-Intelligence
-Competitiveness
-Humor
-Compassion
-Athleticism
-Integrity
-Appearance
-Patience
-Approachability
-Courage
-Self-awareness
-Understanding
-Oratory
-Diplomacy

Obviously, this is an incomplete list and I've left off many attributes. It serves the purpose to spark conversation. It's fascinating watching younger employees work through this list and try to rank them. Every attribute is important for success but some are much more crucial than others. Look at your own prioritization. What did you rank as your top five on this list?

1. _____

2. _____

3. _____

4. _____

5. _____

Now look deeper at my original list on the previous page. What does intelligence mean? Is it academia or "street smarts?" Is it strategic wizardry or tactical excellence? **Humor has played a crucial role in my career** from breaking the ice in new relationships, to distracting people in times of great stress and deadlines. But humor ranges from Ellen De Generis to Chris Rock. Is one better: Perhaps more socially acceptable? I know that I don't personally rank patience high on any list. As my daughter Rosalind points out to me, "Dad, you have a ton of patience--of the "im-kind." I think sometimes that being too patient is a horrid rationalization for accepting something less than you deserve or expect. It can be a cop-out for not taking action when you know inside that you should.

"Let's give this a little more time to see what happens," is not a phrase I ever say, or want to have said to me.

How do you view courage? Are you courageous? Not all of us can be war heroes or pull children from a burning house. However, that doesn't mean that we don't witness acts of courage every day of our life. The working mother of three children who manages to pull off a full -time job, and then get home to make dinner and help with her children's home-work. The devoted father who puts in a rough 40 hour week, and then pulls overtime on Saturday, so he can put away some extra money towards the college fund. I look at Police Officers walking down the street, not getting the respect they deserve. And yet, they are the first people we'd all call in the middle of the night if danger entered our homes. Underpaid teachers forced to deal with a classroom-full of children displaying poor attitudes. Students who disrespect them, threaten them, or physically get in their faces. I'm not sure I'm courageous enough to be a teacher.

I think there is a lot of courage in the world. I also think **you are probably more courageous that you give yourself credit for.**

Go back to my list. What about diplomacy? Now this is an interesting one that causes me to pause. I feel that the majority of people with whom I come into contact are devoid of diplomacy no matter how you define the word. They are two steps away from being Luddites, carry on completely improper conversations and act with the grace of a four-year old throwing a tantrum. Some people with whom I've come across in business seem to misinterpret that diplomacy means manipulation, or being deceitful. Others believe that diplomacy is reserved for he who holds the biggest stick. They are the bullies of the world in business, politics or in the big SUV that just cut you off and gave you the finger.

Diplomacy is much more than being tactful or trying to get the other guy to do what you want him to do. It is the fine art, or dance, between two entities each requiring something from the other. It's the give and take that we all go through every day of our lives. One of my former bosses used to say that diplomacy was treating the other person as if you were wearing gloves. I didn't buy that. On the contrary, over the years I've learned that the art of diplomacy is knowing:

>what to do when the gloves come off

>when to be angry versus when to be calm

>when to stand up versus when to sit down

>when to avoid being hit versus when "not to duck"

Of the above list of attributes, I didn't add "persistence" but given the title of this chapter, I'd be a little worried if you hadn't expected me to discuss it. **I view persistence as the most vital of all attributes in my career success, and that's what I eventually tell anyone who wants to know.**

I know a lot of very intelligent people who probably touch the genius level. Few of them have achieved the kind of success they, or others, felt they deserved because of that intelligence. I know a lot of really approachable, fun people with razor senses of humor who are smart and compassionate. They are all really positive people and I love being with them. If asked if they felt they had achieved their expected levels of success, most would reply a resounding "no."

Working down the list, I've known many outstanding athletes who didn't make the big leagues. I've encountered breathtakingly beautiful people whose looks faded along with their careers.

When I look at the people I know who have made it big in their careers and relationships, there is one key common ingredient they share--persistence. In my estimation, **nothing in the world is more powerful than persistence if it is unleashed against a clear, true and logical objective.** Don't let persistence be mistaken as "mule-headed, stubbornness." You must know your game-plan before you kick you persistence into gear, and you must have identified bail-out actions and time frames in advance. Now, with these in place, and once you have decided on that course of action, it's crucial you begin the process with one question:

"What am I prepared to do?"

I ask this question to my employees, as well as to my two children, when they are approaching a difficult assignment or task.

"What are you prepared to do?" What this really means is:

1. Are you prepared to put in the time investment required to make this project or endeavor a success?

2. Are you prepared to engage help along the way when needed? No man is an island, so don't try to go it alone.

3. Are you prepared to have people tell you that you are wrong and foolish and wasting your time?

4. Are you prepared to anticipate obstacles and determine how to get around, above, under or through them in order to achieve your objectives? Casey Stengel told the press, *"Winning isn't everything, it's the only thing."* His teams won big because he wouldn't let obstacles thwart his determination.

5. Are you prepared to be tired, bored, frustrated and fatigued and still drive forward?

Do you find that people you know are persistent, menacingly persistent, or do they tend to relent and give up? I'd say my answer would be mixed. I continue to witness quitters who retreat the minute they face any substantial opposition. Without fail, out come the excuses and rationalizations. I hate to hear, *"I know I didn't pull it off, but I think in hindsight, I'm in a much better place now because of the outcome."* I'm not sure if this answer is any better or worse than, "It just wasn't worth all the hassle. The result I achieved is just as good." Hmm.

These are the people who are prepared to settle for less and that drives me insane. How can you settle for *"less"* when you could have *"more?"*

I don't care if you are Albert Einstein-smart or your IQ is lower than the room temperature of an igloo. I don't care if you look like Jessica Alba or that blind date that you got set up with in college who looked like Frankenstein's younger sister (but you were told she had a "great personality"). In the long run, none of that matters.

If you hope to achieve the best results in your career and your personal relationships you must immediately bolster you PQ (persistence quotient). Stop letting obstacles and naysayers distract you from your goals and ambitions. Set your game-plan in motion, know it won't be easy, anticipate what might fly at you, and then go for it! Remember that persistence requires friends and allies. Bring your posse into your thinking. Share your goals. It's a lot harder to not deliver when you have broadcast your intent. Engage their help and experience in reaching your objectives.

I'd like to share with you an example of persistence that made all the difference to where I am sitting today. It happened 30 years ago as I am writing this chapter. I was graduating from university and like all of my co-students was racing to find my first real full-time job. In the late 70's, there were lots of jobs...unlike today. Companies came on campus to interview students and then would cull down a list of candidates to bring to their head office for a full day of interviews. I had narrowed down my search to the marketing field and snagged an on-campus interview with General Foods. At that time, GF was considered an outstanding and prominent marketing organization that was reputed as being training-focused and a breeding ground for future CEOs. (GF has since been taken over by Kraft Foods Inc.)

Astoundingly, I made it through the first round and was invited to the Toronto head office of General Foods. GF was going to hire ten students from a probable short-list of forty from all the Canadian business schools. The competition for the job would be stiff so I sat down and took stock of what I had going for me and how I should approach the interview.

1. My grades were average.

2. I knew little about marketing beyond what I had learned in the classroom.

3. I didn't come from Toronto or a private school. I came from small-town Ontario and a family who had no business experience.

4. I had a fun personality and a good sense of humor.

5. I wasn't afraid to work hard and during my summers could show an array of very interesting jobs.

6. I had really good references from those summer jobs.

7. I was persistent in everything I did...once I made my mind up what I was after.

I admit it wasn't the most impressive list. It was then I realized that I had to go as deep as I could to learn about the company and its products. I also had to show them my absolute zeal, professionalism and desire for the job. That's how I had gotten summer jobs in the past. So I prepared as much as the pre-internet world would allow. I went to the library to study annual reports. I went to stores to do shelf checks and pricing analyses. I spoke to a few store managers about General Foods and their sales forces. I spent time with a number of my professors who had worked in the marketing industry. The more I studied my target, the more convinced I became that this job opportunity was an excellent spring-board from which I could launch an entire career. It would be like gaining another degree and a raft of contacts that could help me throughout life. My mindset was focused that the benefits of this particular job, in this specific company and industry, at this particular time would be immeasurable. Aside from just seeking a job, I came to believe that this prospect could be a turning point in my entire life.

Primed with this knowledge, I drove my oil-sucking, egg-shell blue Datsun B-210 to Toronto. I took along my new $99.00 three-piece polyester-based suit and my $19.99 canary yellow "simulated-cotton" button-down shirt. Thank God I knew enough not to stand too close to an open flame with all that synthetic clothing on me.

The Tuesday morning of my all-day interview was abnormally hot for early May with temperatures in the high 80s at 8:00 am. I left my hotel and being new to Toronto, had some minor difficulty in locating and managing the subway. In fact, to that point in my life, I had never been on a subway, or a plane for that matter. My hotel was only minutes away from the head office of General Foods but in my excitement and inexperience, I took the wrong subway and ended up thirty minutes in the opposite direction. When a polite passerby noticed my confusion, he pointed me in the right direction and explained, 'Well son, you do know that the subways go both directions, don't you?"

By now the heat of the day and the prospect of being late for my big show unleashed a flood of sweat that had me drenched head to toe. Even my feet were on fire! I got back on the subway and finally disembarked at the correct subway station. What a sight I must have been, running to get to the reception floor of General Foods. I arrived out of breath at 9:15 am...15 minutes late. I was gasping, dizzy from the heat and I felt like a wet rag-doll. The receptionist looked up over the top of her bifocals. She stared intently at me and gave me a very thorough twice-over. Through a very thick haze of Chantilly-Lace perfume she asked quizzically, "Is it raining outside?"

"No, it's not raining outside," I croaked in a nervous voice, ignoring the sarcasm of her question.

"Why are you so wet?" she asked snidely, with a turned up lip.

"It's a little hot outside and I had some trouble with the subway."

"Trouble with the subway?" she echoed, and I refused to continue her game.

The receptionist took my name and phoned one of the senior marketers who was overseeing the interviewing process for the new hires.

"Yes, Howard Breen is here for you. He's 15 minutes late. Certainly, I'll ask him to have a chair."

She turned to me and directed me to sit down.

"By the way, don't be too embarrassed, but you have something on your collar," she whispered, as I took a seat. She fingered the collar of her blouse to emphasize the point, and location of the issue.

Straining to see what she had noticed, I almost shrieked like a little girl. I must have cut myself shaving at the exact point where my shirt collar rubbed up against my neck. I didn't have "something" on my collar. I had a streak of blood all over the front left collar of my canary-yellow shirt. The polyester material had acted like a sponge and sucked every drop of blood from that tiny nick on my neck. It looked like someone had tried to slice my throat in two.

"For fuck sakes," I growled loudly, my total frustration percolating to the surface. Realizing my gaffe, I looked up to see the silver-haired receptionist's jaw drop to the floor. My hope that I had sworn in my "inside voice" evaporated instantly. I catapulted from my seat and asked frantically, "Where's the washroom, please?"

I reappeared in the reception area at 9:30 am with a piece of scotch tape on my neck. The shirt collar couldn't be cleaned. Blood stains don't like to go away. No amount of soap, rubbing or cursing will bring them out. In the lobby, I met the interview coordinator who did everything but shriek when she saw my shirt collar and my *nouveau-drenched* look. I was still sweating like a stuck pig. In a reprimanding voice that I didn't need to hear, she told me I had missed the first interview which was "not a good start and was I serious about this opportunity?"

From my perspective, the entire day was an unmitigated disaster. I was so self-conscious about my shirt, my lateness and my overall appearance that all of my preparation was for not. I didn't display any amount of "grace under pressure" and by the end of the interviews I wanted to crawl under a rock. I was certain that every GF'er who met me must have thought I was an absolute country bumpkin.

The receptionist gave me a chilly "Good-bye" and I slowly made my way back to the subway. This time I headed in the correct direction. When I returned to the campus I entertained my room-mates with the story, and after a few minutes of self-pitying, I had to laugh. It was so inane that I believed that someday I'd look back at it all and remember it fondly. My room-mate Mark Brennan asked what I was going to do about it.

"Do about it? What the hell do you mean do about it?" I replied incredulously, just itching for a fight.

"Do about the interview, you moron," Mark continued smugly. "Aren't you going to keep at it with them? You told me you really wanted this job. What happened to little Mr. Persistence?"

It really hadn't occurred to me but he was right. I wanted the job. I knew I was behind the eight-ball before I even left for Toronto in my gas-guzzling Datsun. **Why had I been so prepared to give up so easily?**

The next day I phoned General Foods. I spoke with the Marketing Department's director overseeing the hiring process, Rob Dougans. We spoke about my interview day and I shared with him the entire background story. He was very understanding and graciously told me that I actually hadn't done as poorly as I had imagined. I had held my own in the interviews and despite looking like I had been nailed by a vampire, impressed a number of the interviewers with my knowledge of the company and my desire to join them. Unfortunately for me, Rob said that they had their ten hires lined up and he would keep me in mind for a future consideration.

"Really Mr. Dougans," I replied confidently, as I steeled my determination and proclaimed fervently to myself that if it was the last thing I ever did, I was going to be offered a job to start at General Foods. I called back every day for the next two weeks. I spoke with Rob, his assistant, the receptionist in front of whom I had sworn, and any of the other interviewers who would take my calls. I was never rude or inconsiderate. I would get someone on the phone and continue to stress my desire for the job. I would share an idea I had been considering about Maxwell House coffee, Kool-Aid Flavor Crystals or any other GF product that came to mind. I just refused to stand down even if it meant being put on hold for 15 minutes. Remember, this is pre-internet so there was no e-mailing. It was all personal and voice to voice. My persistence would not allow me to *"fade away into that gentle night."*

After my relentless chase, Rob acquiesced, or took pity on me, and I was invited to return to GF to "try again." (His generosity and compassion is something I would never forget, and haven't). I showed up 30 minutes early and brought flowers to the receptionist to apologize for my ungentlemanly outburst in her lobby. I stuck to my original game-plan and ended up laughing with most of the interviewers about my ridiculous first visit to the company. Their willingness to give me a second shot made them all the more appealing. They opened the door and I ran through full-steam.

My persistence paid off and I got the job. It was everything and more than I had imagined. It was a breeding ground of ideas and the training and mentoring that the company promoted was unparalleled. General Foods did serve as the perfect springboard for my career and much to my great fortune I formed a network of incredibly talented individuals from whom I still learn today. This lesson of setting a target and then relentlessly sticking with it became a major part of my personality and business philosophy.

Nothing in my career has ever proven to be more vital to my success than persistence. My reasoning for wanting, and needing, to get that first job at General Foods was proven to be sound. I still look back at it as one of the best training systems I've ever seen. The bosses who helped form the early foundations of my career have all gone on to bigger and better things in life. I'm fortunate to have been able to spend some time with such high quality individuals.

Coincidentally, I saw Rob Dougans the other night at a reception, and we shared a good laugh about my initial interview with General Foods...three decades before. I mentioned I was cobbling together a book and that my interview lesson at GF had once again supported my attitude towards persistence. He told me that throughout his entire career, persistence had made all the difference for him. He said that he often quotes Disraeli in this regard. *"The secret to success is constancy of purpose."*

Chapter 6 Key:

I have learned that nothing in the world is more powerful than persistence in relentlessly pursuing a goal.

Chapter 7

"Get your facts first, then you can distort them as you please….

-Mark Twain

How many times have you proceeded to make a decision or render a conclusion *based on something you thought?* This is what we all do most all the time, correct? That's how we make decisions and form conclusions. Sometimes we believe we have enough information to proceed. Other times, we are missing pieces of the puzzle, but deadlines require us to act. The key phrase in this paragraph is, "based on something you thought."

To some readers this will appear to be a blinding glimpse of the obvious. Good. To the majority of you, it won't. Consider this. When information is being given to you, how do you know if it's factual? You can't always *know that. Try this fictional story on for size.*

A work colleague of yours named Carol Simpson walks by and tells you it's raining outside. You look out your window and can plainly see it is absolutely pouring. A whole array of different colored umbrellas can be seen moving about on the side-walk far below your window. What you were told was factual. You can now form a conclusion on whether or not you need to call a cab for a lunch appointment you have in 45 minutes.

On another day, you are working in a windowless boardroom and have an important lunch appointment uptown in 45 minutes. It's been a long morning and you've been stuck in that boardroom for over three hours. When you got up this morning, you were listening to the radio and heard the announcer calling for thunderstorms throughout the day. Your colleague Carol walks by the boardroom door and waves hello at you. You smile and ask her if it's raining outside. She shakes her head "no" and confirms it's a beautiful day outside. This is great to hear so you bide your time knowing you can walk to your lunch appointment. It will take about 15 minutes. However, when you exit your building, much to your surprise, and shock, you discover it is pouring rain. The sky is black with thunderclouds and it's lightening like never before. Someone standing at the door mentions that it's been like this for over two hours. You try to call a cab on your cell-phone but there is the obvious backload of callers. They can't get to you for 35 minutes. Steaming at Carol for the bad information, you borrow an umbrella from the security desk and head out into the torrential downpour. At the first corner, a Lincoln Navigator drives by. As its front right tire catches the edge of a six inch puddle, it sends a spray of water into the air catching you from the waist down. You are drenched. It takes another twenty minutes for you to arrive at your lunch. There is not a dry spot on your entire body. You are late and you look like a drowned rat. Your appointment is furious for having to wait and already ordered his lunch. What a great way to start off an important meeting.

What happened? It is the same colleague. We're you lied to? Why did Carol Simpson answer falsely? How could she have made such a basic mistake? You need to find out the answer but the net of it is that your lunch is an unmitigated disaster.

Face the first fact that any fault is yours, not Carols. As it turns out, Carol is a very good colleague and likes you a lot. She would never knowingly steer you wrong. Carol arrived at the office when the sun was shining and there was nary a cloud in the sky. From entering the building, she was in a windowless boardroom down the hall from you. She hadn't passed any windows when you asked her the question. Carol hadn't heard the weather report calling for rain so when you asked her about the weather, everything told her it was a nice day. Carol didn't mean to mislead you. She should have said, "It was a beautiful day when I arrived an hour ago. I'm not sure about it now." But she didn't. Nor did you ask her for any clarification.

"Oh, I had heard it was going to rain," you might have said to her. "I'm just about to head out for a lunch date. Did you just come in from outside?"

Wouldn't that have been a smart thing to do? Carol clarifies that her information is an hour old. You leave the boardroom and get to an office where you can look outside. Good Lord, it's pouring, I need a cab. Not quite rocket science.

The difference I'm muddling through in this overly-simplified example is in **knowing something for a fact, versus believing something to be true.** Sometimes, it's the same thing when you don't have your facts in order. The vast majority of time, *it is not.* Ronald Reagan said that, *"facts are stubborn things."*

I drill this mantra into my children's heads by repeating the question whenever they are telling me something. "Honey, is this something you know or believe?"

You should ask this question (without the endearment) numerous times daily. If you aren't clarifying the validity of information being given to you, then you are raising the risk of making a false conclusion. With Carol, you ended up getting wet and buggering up a lunch appointment. Not a serious price in the long run. Now, shall we take this to a different level?

Let's position this as a possible career terminating situation on a decision you have to make based on information you have been given.

Michael McKelvey is a colleague at the office. You are both in the same position in different divisions. He seems like a good guy, trustworthy and well-meaning. Every couple of weeks you grab lunch with him and catch up on family, and company gossip. One Thursday morning in May, Michael arrives at your office, comes in and quietly closes the door. An air of mystery and tension immediately permeates the room.

"Hey Mike, what's going on?" you ask, pushing away from the desk.

"I wasn't sure whether to tell you something I heard this morning in the lobby," he begins. "It's not really pleasant and I don't want you to shoot the messenger."

"What did you hear?" you ask anxiously, as your heart-beat picks up its pace.

"I overheard your boss Doug telling Steve Samson in Accounting that he was really ticked off with you for being so late on the Nike file he gave you last week. Doug said it was due yesterday and you hadn't finished it. I heard your boss say he was considering replacing you."

"Replacing me," you blurt out loudly, before quieting yourself. "Did Doug say I was being fired?"

"I didn't hear the word *fired,* but that's the meaning I took from it," Michael responds vehemently. "You need to drop everything you are doing and get that file into your boss a.s.a.p. or you're finished here."

Michael seems to be very sincere in what he is telling you. He looks disturbed and genuinely concerned for your well-being. He didn't have to share this information with you, and you <u>are</u> late on a report he knew nothing about. The time had disappeared and before you could finish the first job, your boss Doug had given you a second task to complete. It was on Microsoft and had an incredibly important deadline tomorrow morning at 9:00 am sharp. It was worth close to a million dollars in revenue to the company.

"Well, the only way I can get the Nike file done today is to drop everything I'm doing and then pull an all-nighter on Microsoft to get it done by 9:00 am tomorrow," you remonstrate, hoping Michael has a solution. "Even that might bugger up the Microsoft project because I won't be able to get all of the pertinent data I need." You can hear the sharpening of the guillotine blade somewhere in the recesses of your brain.

"All I know is that your boss is really angry and I'd get that Nike file underway and on his desk today," he concludes obstinately as he turns and leaves your office. "Good luck pal."

Have you faced one of these situations before?

In this case, you have no real reason to doubt the information supplied by Michael. Your boss does have a real temper and in the past hasn't been shy about terminating his employees. He did give you the Nike file last week and you are late and didn't tell him. What do you do? Here are some options:

1. Ignore what Michael has told you and complete the Microsoft file to meet tomorrow's deadline at 9:00 am. Then, get onto the Nike file at 9:05 am and hand it in before close of business that day.

2. Listen to your colleague and pull an all-nighter to get both files completed...the Nike today by 5:00 pm and the Microsoft tomorrow by 9:00 am.

3. Listen to Michael and drop what you are doing to get the Nike file done now. Nothing is more important than removing the risk of being fired. Once this Nike file is completed, your boss will not have grounds to dismiss you. Try to get an extension on the Microsoft file until later the next day.

4. None of the above.

The more senior you are in your career, the higher the chances are that you selected #4 or #1 as your course of action. The more junior, and less battle-worn you are, the greater the probability you chose another answer. Here's what I'd ask you to consider in sorting out the correct course of action. First, when faced with this situation, don't show emotion or concern to the messenger. While they may be "losing their head to emotion," you must not. Second, have them repeat exactly what they heard. Ask if they are paraphrasing or using exact words. How did they manage to hear this? Who else was around who might be able to corroborate the discussion? What was the situation surrounding the discussion? **Don't accept information without probing for more details.** This is a perfect example of you being forced to make a decision without knowing if the information is factual, or only a belief.

This story, with different clients and people involved, happened to me. It was like being hit with a ton of bricks. My career flashed before my eyes. I realized that there was only one valid course of action. I needed to go directly to the source. No beating around the bush. My boss was an unpleasant type who didn't like un-scheduled drop-ins. No "open door policy" for him. If I was going to be fired then I needed to know it then and there. Don't ever mess around with speculation or hearsay. Take charge, get the facts and face the music. Here is how you should handle the situation above on the Nike and Microsoft files. Firstly, go directly to your boss.

"Doug, got a minute?" you ask standing in his doorway.

"What? I'm really busy," he answers sharply, without looking up from his papers. "Come back later."

"I can't. This is really important," you continue deliberately, and take a few steps into the room. Doug finally looks up and shrugs his shoulders, which to the rest of the world means, **"what?"**

"I need to confirm that I'm doing the right thing. I'm going full steam ahead to make tomorrow morning's Microsoft deadline. That's meant that I just haven't been able to complete last week's Nike file. I put it off until I could get Microsoft in order."

Doug sits back in his chair and tilts his head quizzically.

"And you are telling me this because..." he asks, emphasizing each word in that annoying way only he can muster.

"We'll, I realized I hadn't told you I was going to be late on last week's file and I didn't want to let you down."

"You aren't letting me down," he counters firmly, as he stands up and leans against his desk. He looks slightly puzzled. "You will be letting me down if you screw up the Microsoft deadline. I knew you couldn't get both projects done. Just yesterday I asked Steve Samson if he had some capacity on his team to lend you a hand on the other file. Even I know that you can't be expected to do two things that big all in the same timeframe." He cracks a slight smile at his last statement.

You quietly sigh in relief. "So you aren't ticked about the Nike file?"

"No, what gave you that idea?" he replies nonchalantly, as he re-takes his seat and returns to his papers. His action signifies that the meeting is over and you are dismissed.

Can you see how ugly this could have gone by pursuing the other options? Throughout your career, you will have many situations arise that will not be too different from this example with Michael and Doug. You will have only partial information and unmovable deadlines. Be en garde for well-meaning messengers who bring you data that is nothing more than a red-herring. You must not be distracted from the logic of the situation. **When in doubt, go directly to the source, or to your supervisor, and get the factual information.**

Don't ever over-react to disturbing information. Immobilize your emotions. To borrow a saying my mother-in-law uses, *"chest your cards."*

Size up the intent behind the words/data and don't be so gullible as to accept everything you are told. **Don't make decisions without trying your utmost to discern fact from belief.**

One last caution for you to consider: I've witnessed people make wrong decisions based on information that was not factual. It was however, information they were hoping to hear. Information they wanted to be real. Information they "needed" to be real, even when it wasn't. George Orwell, writer of "*1984*" and "*Animal Farm*" wrote, *"We are all capable of believing things which we know to be untrue, and then, when we are finally proved wrong, impudently twisting the facts so as to show that we were right."*

The results of doing this can be catastrophic and globally altering. We've all see this in the very recent past.

"Bush. Iraq. Weapons of mass destruction." Oops.

Chapter 7 Key:

You either know something or you believe it. Make it the former and your success will increase dramatically. Try to turn the facts into what you want them to say and you'll regret it. Remember to worry about what you can change, not what you can't.

Chapter 8

"Oh, so you hate your job? Why didn't you say so? There's a support group for that. It's called EVERYBODY, and they meet at the bar…"

-Drew Carey

People ranging from graduating students to Presidents of large companies ask me how to find the job that's right for them. Ironically, it can be just as difficult for an employed President to snare his/her ideal job as it is for the new graduate to receive their first employment offer.

Let's review some thought starters that apply to anyone, currently employed, or otherwise. Your level of seniority is irrelevant in this discussion.

1. Be selective in the job you wish to have. Don't take a job just for the money, unless you have no other choice. Confucius said, *"Choose a job you love and you will never work a day in your life."*

2. Ensure you have completed Chapter 1 which will help you to clarify what it is you actually want to be doing.

3. Realize that **finding and securing the correct job for you is not something you can do alone.** You need to mobilize every contact and relationship you have. You need to set aside any apprehension in asking people for help in identifying leads, or perhaps even opening a door for an interview.

4. Determining what you should be doing is not an easy task. You need to investigate all industries and talk to a variety of different people. If you only talk to people in the marketing world…then you'll only learn about the marketing world.

5. Understand the role that geography will play in your decision. Is it vital that you remain in your current city or country for family, or personal reasons? Flexibility in geography can open a new world of opportunities. There's life beyond North America and it's exciting.

6. **Don't put all your eggs into one basket.** Don't lock and load on one industry, or one company. Create "springboards" of opportunities utilizing your network of contacts and people with whom you interview.

7. Keep a meticulously written daily journal of all activities and analyses you are working through. Document every phone call and conversation.

8. Resumes are almost a waste of time unless you can get what needs to be said in about 15 seconds worth of reading. However, tradition dictates a resume so keep yours factual, honest and brief. Don't pull a George O'Leary, the short-lived coach of Notre Dame University who after 5 days on his new job was removed for falsifying his resume.

9. After narrowing down a number of industries, locations and potential companies, **go really deep to know where you want to be employed:**

   -Research the industry and all major competitors by reading industry magazines, annual reports, analysts' reports, blogs, web-sites and financial sections in the press. Learn about the major players running these companies through Google and Wikipedia. Build a file on exactly for whom you would be working.

   -Contact the receptionist and secure the names of the last ten hires brought into the company. Research their backgrounds as noted above. This will help you to ensure that the qualities and skill sets the company is seeking are in parallel with your own. Now, call those new employees and ask for 5 minutes on the phone to help you learn how they got the job. Ask if the company has delivered what it promised.

10. **Physically visit the companies you have targeted when employees are arriving and/or leaving work.** Do they appear happy? Are they laughing and hanging out with each other? Do they look friendly or haggard? These will be your co-workers and you need to determine if the environment fits your style.

Enter the building and hang out in the reception/lobby area for a half an hour. What message does the reception area send you? Ask the receptionist about her job. Casually investigate the mood of the place. What's the dress code and what should you be wearing for your interviews.

11. Once you've completed your preliminary scouting investigation, narrow down your top 3-5 options and go deep. Find out who conducts the interviewing. Check them out (as per Point 9) on Google, Facebook and LinkedIN and build backgrounders on them all. I haven't mentioned Recruiting firms or Headhunters to this point. I've had great success hiring through these firms. I've had some misses. Don't depend on them to find you a job. You must **use all your contacts.** You can use them to help you get backgrounders and potentially to set up an interview. Remember, if you can avoid being placed by a recruiting firm and orchestrate a "direct interview/hire," it saves the company money. Perhaps this could be negotiated as part of your salary.

12. Let's review what happens once you have secured the interview. You have meticulously completed very thorough backgrounders on everyone you will be meeting. You've given considered thought to the company and why it is right for you...and why you are right for them. With your network, you have prepared potential questions that may/should arise, along with responses that you have repeatedly practiced and rehearsed. I often tell people, at all levels of seniority, to rehearse in front of a mirror or with the aid of a camcorder. **These rehearsals will make all the difference in the world with how well you communicate exactly what you intend say.** They will also help you in your physical representation and delivery.

13. Arrive to the building 30 minutes before the interview and walk up to the lobby with 15 minutes to spare. Being late is a deal breaker unless you've been in a 10 car pile-up and you have an ugly bloody bone sticking out through your shirt. Turn off anything electronic that you are carrying including cell-phones and Blackberries. Come fully prepared with writing materials, along with your backgrounder on the company. Have 2-3 extra resumes with you. Don't assume that the people interviewing you will remember much from your resume, if in fact they've even read it.

Another critical point to remember is to **treat every interviewer individually.** Simply because you've received answers to your questions during the first interview doesn't mean you don't repeat the questions to every person who interviews you. First, they may have different answers and you need to be looking for information and consistency. Secondly, they will form opinions of you based on the quality and depth of your questions. There is nothing worse than hearing an interviewee say to me, "No, I don't have any more questions. They've all been answered."

14. **First impressions are vital.** Regardless of your title, don't ever forget this: Direct eye contact and a firm handshake. Manners and politeness should be coming naturally. Always begin the meeting by confirming how much time you have with the interviewer. Feel comfortable to take brief notes during the talk. Don't ramble and *don't be coy.* Answer questions thoughtfully, and thoroughly. I often end my answer with, "Have I answered your question fully enough?"

15. Target for the 50/50 rule in sharing the conversation and questions. Help the interviewer get to know you so (s)he can make a concerted decision if you fit the bill. Part of this information exchange is the caliber and intelligence of the questions that you bring to the table. Given that you've already researched the interviewer, you should be able to use that information to make your questions all the more interesting and relevant. Similarly, the interviewer has to help you to understand the role, accountabilities, culture and opportunity so that you have enough information to decide if the job is right for you...and vice versa. At the end of the day, it's really you who stands the better chance of deciding if the marriage "will work."

16. I always encourage people to **err on the side of formality in first meetings,** but I also suggest that they be interesting and engaging. Ensure that you've read the morning's newspapers, and your favorite on-line news service. See what you can scoop to use in the discussion. Make sure you have visited the company's web-site the morning of your interview.

17. If you are offered a drink, take it. If the interviewer has to go to a kitchen to pick it up, go with them. Every minute counts and you will also get to see how other employees react to your interviewer.

18. Alright, let's move to the next step. Your meetings are over, and you are very encouraged about the prospects of the job. Now, the dance begins. You must follow up with each person...but

you must not appear overly anxious. That can be interpreted as being desperate, or willing to take a lower salary to get the job. I would suggest a very neatly <u>handwritten</u> note to each person that interviewed you. I would thank them, include something I had learned from their meeting, and perhaps mention an idea that the interview sparked. For the more senior ranks, I would recommend that you include the names of several people you share in common with the lead interviewer. Include their phone numbers and suggest that a call might be in order. (For Goodness sakes, pre-warn these people that a call might be coming and give them information on the firm, the position, and why you would be a good hire). If possible, you should hand-deliver these notes to the receptionist at the company. Do not mail them. Do not send an e-mail. Be personable in this. Your thank-you notes should arrive on their desks the day following the interview.

18. Two weeks following your meetings, call the assistant of the lead interviewer and schedule a ten minute phone call. It is perfectly reasonable to determine the status of the interviewing process and to believe that other candidates are being seen. At this point it is also acceptable to send an e-mail (or two) with a worthwhile idea which might help grow the company.

19. A number of "career experts" warn against following up. I disagree. I don't want candidates to be rude or insensitive to my time pressures, but I do want to see tenacity and creativity in how they manage to keep me thinking about them. If I can't see their ability to sell themselves to me...then how will they ever help to grow my company?

20. **Maintain a positive and optimistic attitude no matter how many doors get shut in your face.** Interviewers can smell fear and trepidation in their candidates.

Chapter 8 Key:

If you are not happy with your job then get your act in gear and find a new one. It will be hard work and you'll have lots of doors closed in your face. Tough it out but don't stay in a job you hate.

Chapter 9

"We must be the change we wish to see…"

-Gandhi

You are in your 30s or early 40s, and your contemporaries are passing you by. Your career has stalled. One by one, your peers are getting promotions and new accountabilities. You can only imagine how their remuneration is outpacing your own. They seem to get invited to meetings that you hear about after the fact. You job responsibilities haven't changed and your last raise was marginal. In your opinion, your peers aren't bringing any more to the table than are you. They certainly aren't smarter and don't work any longer hours? So then, why are they are getting all the breaks? How do you rectify this and kick your career back into high gear? Is it possible at your current company, or do you need to be considering a change in companies to get your career back on track?

These are all good questions that must be answered. First, let's start by establishing facts. Your opinion will not be objective. **You can't help but bias your own interpretation on your abilities and contribution versus other employees.** We are all amazing little *rationalizers* when it comes right down to it. Write down what you know to be facts. List your peers and their progression through the company with any changes to their titles, number of direct reports and office location/size. Do the same for yourself. Ensure you compare tenure. List the supervisors of each peer and rank them within the company. Are any reporting directly to the President…while you aren't? Now, add to your list the amount of interaction each of you, and your peers, have with the two most senior officers in your division or overall, in the company.

It's time for the gut-wrenching reality check. How does your list look? Are you near the top and simply over-reacting with a little too much sensitivity, *or* are your suspicions valid? We'll proceed with the fact that your suspicions were not made up, and you weren't negatively biasing the situation. Here's how you might consider proceeding. *"Houston, we have a problem."*

Do you have the requisite "trusted confident" in the senior ranks of the organization? Go and talk with them. See what you can learn. If you can get the straight dope, you'll save yourself a lot of angst and wasted time. There can be a dozen reasons, both fair and unfair as to why you are being passed over. You need to uncover these reasons and determine if it's possible for you to rectify the situation at this company. If it's too late and you are toast, then you need to learn from this situation to be able to address it in your next company. Don't just pack up and look for a new job. You'll find yourself in the same situation in very short order if you don't understand what happened.

Without a senior level confidant you need to tackle this somewhat differently. Have you had a formal, written evaluation within the last 6-12 months? If yes, pull it out and analyze it in great depth to see what you might not have fully understood. Did the evaluation outline "development needs" that you've been trying to address? Do you have physical proof/documentation of how you've been succeeding? Would your boss agree with this "proof?" I'll wager the answer is no.

If you've not received a formal written evaluation, then send a note to your supervisor requesting one. Copy the head of the Human Resources department on your letter. If you do not have a thoroughly written job description, then request that one be included in the evaluation. Suggest a time-frame and what you are hoping to learn from the evaluation in order to improve your performance, and make you a more valuable employee for the company. (By the way, shame on you if you don't have a written job description. The most junior people in the company should have one).

Several outcomes to your request are possible. It's up to you to understand how you intend to react to each outcome. It's a positive sign if your supervisor agrees to your request and conducts the evaluation. Approach the review with a positive attitude and an open mind. You want to hear everything (s)he knows, and perceives about your performance. You want the good, the bad and the ugly. Come prepared with examples of your work, any notes on feedback you've received from your boss, co-workers, clients etc. Don't show up to the meeting empty-handed. Come to the meeting with suggestions for training you feel you are missing; and ideas on over and above projects you might be able to take on to help your supervisor and the company. Don't arrive at the meeting with a chip on your shoulder and the attitude of "Hey I'm being left behind and I demand to know why." Approach this evaluation intending to learn everything possible...whether you end up staying or leaving the company.

At the actual evaluation meeting listen carefully and take notes. Probe for examples if there are concerns raised about your performance. Ensure you understand the accountabilities on your plate. Don't be defensive. Encourage complete candor and honesty. Ask what more you can be doing to fulfill your role. Is there a next job for you at this company? Go ahead and ask that question. If there's humming and hawing, you have your answer. If there is upside for you then understand exactly what you have to deliver and display to make it to the next level. What timing is involved? What training and development program should you investigate?

If your supervisor facilitates a proper evaluation, you should have a perfect picture as to exactly where you stand. You should know your strengths and weaknesses with examples of each.

What if your supervisor agrees to conduct an evaluation but it's not forthcoming? You remind him/her yet months continue to pass without anything happening? Well, that in itself is a major confirmation of your suspicions that something in your career at your company is amiss. At this point you can:

- decide to play "ostrich" and continue showing up at work. You should believe your days are numbered and eventually you are going to be asked, "Got a minute?"

- let your supervisor off the hook and not raise it again but get your resume on the street and proceed to find yourself a new job.

- resign and move on. Remember, it's always better to find a new position while you are employed.

There is another option. I don't generally like the "ostrich" approach. You are never going to learn what you did, or didn't do, to be passed over. How will you avoid falling into the same traps in your next role? You must find out what has transpired at your company. Go at the issue harder. Personally, I would send a note to my supervisor and copy his/her boss and the head of Human Resources/Personnel. My note would read like this:

"My formal request for a written evaluation is being ignored and put off. I need feedback in order to be the best employee I can for this company. If there are issues I need to address at work, then how can I be expected to do that without an evaluation? Again, I formally request an evaluation and a written job description (if you don't have one)."

There is the slim possibility that you are okay and the supervisor has been lax in putting off your evaluation. If this is the case, you will see a meeting booked in due order. However, the opposite is highly likely. **If you have been marked by your superiors as being a marginal performer with limited upside you are about to find out. Wouldn't you rather find out so you can take control of the situation and your career?** There is nothing more damaging to your health and well-being that living in uncertainty and angst that something is wrong...but not knowing for certain. If you are honestly giving your 100% effort, and have brought the right team-attitude to your company, then you have a right to know the truthful status of your longevity.

In *"The World is Flat"* author Thomas L. Friedman states, *"If there is a new social contract implicit between employers and employees it should be this: You give me your labor, and I will guarantee that as long as you work here, I will give you every opportunity-through either career advancement or training-to become more employable, more versatile."*

Is this how you view your contract with your employer? Do you believe that this is how they view you?

Understand that not all employees are A+ performers. Jack Welch ran General Electric utilizing an approach called "20/70/10" where 100% of all employees were ranked as being superior/average to above average/no advancement. Companies need the 20s and 70s to make the operations successful. They need to have the 10s gone...preferably without an expensive severance. You may fall into the lower 70s group, or perhaps even the 10s. As such, the company may be prepared to let you continue as an employee but have already labeled you as having a limited potential. They may also be biding their time to avoid a severance or to find the right person to take over your accountability. Either way, **if you've been moved to the back burner, *you need to know.***

I've seen all of the above cases at every company where I've worked. When asked my counsel, I regularly tell people in this situation of being *passed over* to:

a) determine if it's factually true;

b) determine exactly why it happened;

c) judge if it is fixable; and,

d) get their house in order and be prepared to find a new job.

Your career is your career. Don't leave it in the hands of your employer. **Keep your fingers on the pulse of how you are perceived in the organization, not how you believe you are performing.** Keep track of how well your supervisors are doing in the organization and try your best to work for the best teachers and the "rising stars." Make yourself invaluable to them and grab hold of their jacket when they move up the ladder. Take care not to be associated with, or working for, a supervisor who's being moved out of the company. You may find yourself considered collateral damage and end up being terminated as well.

Chapter 9 Key:

You are in charge of your career, not the company for whom you work. If something appears amiss--then don't play ostrich. Get the straight goods and determine if it's fixable and what you need to do. Take charge of your career.

Chapter 10

"I do not know anyone who has got to the top without hard work. That is the recipe. It will not always get you to the top, but it should get you pretty close..."

-Margaret Thatcher 1985

As a CEO, I'm being overwhelmed with the expectations of the younger hires coming into the company. In their twenties, this group has arrived with incredible levels of over-inflated self worth. A watermelon-sized ego is coupled with little experience, or proven success. This is an issue plaguing business far beyond the advertising industry in Canada, or the States. It's an issue hurting the competitiveness of business in general. I realize that most companies have not done a good job in endearing themselves to their employees in such a manner to deserve loyalty in return. On the contrary, it seems that most companies do the opposite. Younger employees making up the next generation of our workforce are arriving with false expectations of what they deserve, and what they are prepared to do to get ahead. Careers seem to be considered passé with a good number of these workers planning to jump from job to job as the opportunities arise. To hell with longevity, or the investment of time. I personally have worked for 7 companies in my career to date. I'm not averse to the grabbing of opportunities. My career has spanned 3 decades. I'm seeing a plethora of resumes of employees having worked at 7 companies in ten years! That's ludicrous.

Are our universities and colleges coddling their students and ingraining them with false pretenses about the workforce? Has the business world been so abusive to its workforce that this backlash was inevitable? **Why is it that many of the younger work-force adamantly refuses to invest their time to drive their careers with over and above**

duties? Our younger employees seem to only want to work 9-5 and the thought of overtime is blasphemy. We've had employees arrive at our Human Resources department at month 3 demanding a salary review. We have actually had a number of these same junior employees ask for promotions. After 3 months!

This group I'm discussing is multi-labeled Gen Y, Echo Boomers, Internet Generation, Nintendo Generation or the Digital kids, and they are an intriguing breed. Driven to the internet and connectivity with their friends, they love to travel and learn. Giving consideration to a career, as opposed to a short term job, doesn't seem to fit their bill. How does this mindset fit today's companies?

Well, I'm concerned how it fits when I read about Canada continually falling in the rankings of competitiveness on a global scale. However, I understand this deterioration because I'm seeing it first-hand. I wonder how much of an employee's actual working day is spent on the company's business rather than surfing the internet on Facebook or MySpace.com. To a good number of employees, I wonder if the company is really anything more than a bi-monthly paycheck, and a medical plan. The slippage in attitude of wanting to invest to get ahead has become epidemic in business. The younger employees who actually put in the extra hours really do stand out wonderfully from the crowd. Their attitude is refreshing and their thinking and ideas help companies be successful and grow. These go-getters will get the salary raises and promotions. They will be earmarked for special assignments and training. Do recognize however, that the backlash to their successes from their contemporaries is instant.

"Why them and not me?" is the constant refrain. "I'm doing my job and working hard." In the well-conceived book, *"Balance of Power,"* James R. Lucas writes about entitlement:

"They think they are entitled not to have to think about profit and loss, product or service viability, long range plans, or the impact of their performance (good or bad) on the health of the organization. When pay and benefits have to be restrained or cut, the wails go up: "Wait a minute we're entitled to those things." And when demands for individuals to take more responsibility and have more accountability for results are made, the wails go up again: "That's management's job, not mine."

There are a lot of people who share this attitude about life. Not all of them are Generation Y'ers. However, this sentiment, written more than a decade ago by Lucas, seems to aptly apply to the newest faces entering the working world.

Woody Allen was wrong in thinking that *"Eighty percent of success is just showing up."* So are you if that's your philosophy in life. Showing up isn't even the ante.

Am I being too harsh? What is your experience in the working world? Perhaps I'm just too "old school" and know the intensity of effort that I made in my career. I try to look at this as objectively as I can. As such, I decided to go back to square one and compare what expectations the employee was justified in having of his/her employer versus expectations the employer should have of each employee. I think these expectations are universal and cross all industries. Ironically as you read this, you'll see that in this book the employee has the right to expect more.

A. What are the just demands that I as an employee should have of my employer?

1. **A safe working environment.** I should not have to worry about my health in any way. I should never feel pressured because of my age, sexuality, race or religion.

2. A clearly **written job description** that outlines: my accountabilities; the company's expectations of me; the action standards against which I will be evaluated; the hierarchy of my reporting structure; the vehicle outlining how I will be evaluated on an annual basis; the company's policies to which I must adhere; the system of how my needs can be communicated back to the company; and, the process of how my career is expected to advance through the organization (including a training approach).

3. **To be treated with respect** by all other company employees, clients/customers of the company, and suppliers to the company.

4. **Fair pay for work done.** My salary should reflect industry standards and should be raised commensurate with my tenure

and my contribution.

5. **Communication** from the most senior leaders in the organization to help me understand the performance of the company and its game-plan for the future.

6. **Leadership** that upholds the **integrity** of the company at all times with a displayed attitude that employees are more than simply numbers on a financial statement. **Leadership that believes in fair play, respect for the individual and decency** in all company policies and actions.

7. An environment that encourages, and helps me to be the best person I can be. This will mean an understanding by the company that I need a **proper balance between work and my non-working hours.** I understand that there will be times when I'm expected to work overtime when a real crunch period faces the company. I will play my part. What must not happen is the attitude that my entire life is based around the company and they can demand that I continually work beyond my normal working hours. That is not just, and it abusive to my well-being and health. If I've been requested to put in considerable overtime then something must come back "my way." It can be an extra day off, or a bump in my paycheck. My investment in overtime must not be taken for granted. My company should know that my "non-work time" is vital for my physical, mental and emotional health and the investment I'm able to bring to my job every day. **The more balanced my life, the better the longer term contribution I will make to my company.**

B. What are the just demands that I as an employer should have of every employee?

1. Integrity and honesty in all actions at all times.

2. Adherence to all company policies and procedures.

3. The delivery of the job accountabilities.

4. The desire to improve, to learn and to be the best employee and person possible.

5. To help the company grow and succeed.

6. A positive winning attitude with a team approach and desire to go the extra mile.

7. The employee's best effort day in and day out with the ability to bring new thinking and ideas to the job.

You'll notice that I have not included the expectation of "loyalty." Don't companies have a right to demand loyalty of their employees? Most companies I know don't treat their employees in such a way to deserve full loyalty. In fact, I heard the CEO of a large multi-national refer to his employees as "serfs." He was not kidding. I almost fell off my chair. When the P+L called for a pull-back on revenue, he ordered that staffing be instantly cut to maintain the proper financial ratios of salaries to revenue. He didn't show any reluctance in the least. Tell me, does he have the right to demand loyalty from his "serfs?" Do the CEOs who have been arrested for pulling fast money games on their organizations causing legions of investors to lose their life savings have the right to demand loyalty from their employees? *Hardly.*

When then does a CEO, as an employer, have the right to demand the loyalty of his/her employees? Of course, a CEO has the right to demand that employees shouldn't blatantly be disloyal by using competitive products or breaching company policies. However, loyalty reaches much further than breaching company policies. I submit that CEOs have the right to expect *true loyalty, if they can answer affirmatively to every one of the following questions.*

1. Your financials have weakened and your bottom line is soft. You must immediately remove either 5% of your total employee cost or eliminate your personal bonus and cut your own salary by 10% for the next year. Would you give serious consideration to the latter option?

2. Do you make an effort to know the names of the majority of your employees?

3. Do you know the names of your 15 most senior employees' significant others?

4. Do you know the name of the person who delivers your mail?

5. Since becoming CEO, have you seriously upgraded the training

and education programs offered to your employees?

6. Do you ever read any exit interviews to see why employees are leaving your company?

7. Do you encourage and even enforce holidays being taken by your employees?

8. Is the employee turnover in your company lower than the industry average?

9. Do you personally meet all new employees?

10. Have you publicly communicated your vision for the company to your employees?

11. Have you implemented clearly defined job descriptions and evaluation procedures for every employee?

12. Do you look at fair pay for work done across all employees?

If as an executive in a company you can honestly answer yes to these questions then you "get it" and deserve a hearty congratulations. You should expect fair play and loyalty in return, from your employees. You are also a rarity in today's leadership circles. I'd wager that the majority of CEOs would have trouble with more than 50% of the questions. Even so, they would be shocked at why they don't deserve loyalty in return.

Chapter 10 Key:

The balance between employer and employee expectations needs to be clearly depicted in writing before the first day you start a new job. Don't leave room for confusion either way. Employees are not all the same. They come from different generations with different expectations and abilities. It's vital that companies recognize these differences if they are to remain competitive.

Chapter 11

"If a man does his best then what else is there?"

-George S. Patton

Half-Hearted efforts and lame excuses make me sick. Giving up before the game is over…if there is one ounce of a chance of pulling off a victory…is a sin. Accepting defeat and being referred to as a good loser is not something of which to be proud. I fervently believe in Vince Lombardi's statement, *"show me a gracious loser, and I'll show you a loser."*

When I was a kid, most members of my immediate family "disliked" playing games or sports with me. Okay, perhaps the word "disliked" is a little too gentle. They out and out hated it. I played every game like there was no tomorrow and that my life depended on it. I must admit that I was, and am, a horrible loser. It drives me insane to lose. When I do lose, there is nothing gracious about me because there is nothing gracious about losing. There is grace in victory. Not in defeat.

Even today, I spend endless hours after any loss, even a card game, replaying the entire event in my head. Heaven help me if I lose at Bridge. I'll be up all night going through every hand, card and bid. I cannot get to sleep until I can determine the errors I had made and how I'll rectify them if faced with the same situation.

As a youngster, I had more heart than skill/talent in most sports I played. I was smaller than most of the kids, and I didn't gain any real height, weight or muscle until I was in Grade 11. Accelerating through Grade 2 had its real drawbacks when it came to sports in later years. I spent a lot of time warming the bench, watching my team-mates play. I got picked last for teams more times than I can remember. It frustrated the living hell out of me. It still stings me when I think about it.

As the years passed, I watched and I learned from the bench, or the side-line. I studied the flow of the game and learned to predict how the tactics would unfold. **I learned that the strategy of the game was more important than simply being the hero who sank the basket, got the triple, spiked the ball, or served the most aces.** The game was about knowing the rules and limitations, and how to work within, and around them. I wasn't as smart as Walter Gretzky who taught Wayne *"not to go to where the puck was but to where it was going to go."* I was smart enough to realize that without any size or real talent, I better understand the machinations of the strategy of any game I intended to play. I also realized that to make any team, I was going to have to have a hell of a lot more desire to win than the next guy.

In my early teens, I determined three vital factors that changed my entire approach to High School sports, university and my career.

1. The best player on the team is not necessarily the strongest, biggest, oldest or the smartest;

2. Some players on the team may have incredible skills and physical prowess but don't necessarily put out their best effort throughout the entire match; and,

3. An unrelenting desire to win coupled with a relentless approach to achieving that desire will steal a victory where a defeat was the most probable outcome.

Think about these three factors for a moment and tell me if you don't agree. How do these factors play into your personal and professional lives today? Do you play on teams with people who aren't giving their best day in and day out? Have you determined who the best players are in your company? Are you separating the shirkers from your stars? How are you helping the shirkers to either improve their efforts and contribution, or get the hell out of your company? What are you doing to retain your stars and put them into positions where they can drive the success of your company?

What about your family members, friends, co-workers or employees? Do any of them fall into the two buckets of weak efforts and lousy excuses? I guarantee your answer is affirmative. In all of our lives, including mine, we must deal with people who just refuse to give their best. We are also subjected to people who come at us with B.S. lame excuses. These people must be dealt with if you are to personally succeed.

If you accept lame excuses and half-hearted efforts from people around you, then you are condoning this behavior which places you in the same dirty bucket. It sends out a message to people watching you that you find this behavior to be acceptable. It also indicates that you engage in this behavior as well. I've heard Richard Peddie, President and CEO of Maple Leaf Sports and Entertainment state on numerous occasions that, *"Leaders get the behavior they exhibit and tolerate."* Condoning these actions means that as a senior executive you will accept less than someone's best and that you personally don't tend to give your 100% best effort. Is this how you want to be viewed? Absolutely not. You want to be surrounded by winners who also want you to be a player on their team. Your want partners who will go for the jugular of anyone who takes a run at you, or your team. You want highly successful go-getters who want you to be on their "A" list.

When people around you shirk their roles/duties, or try to pass off a lame excuse for poor performance, I suggest that you take an immediate and firm stance. Hear them out totally and ask questions to ensure you have the complete picture. And then call the person on the spot. They have no right to insult your intelligence or your own accountabilities by conducting themselves in this manner. They have no right to negatively hamper your, or the company's reputation. Do they believe you to be so stupid that you can't see through their chicanery? If you do not immediately take a frontal stance with these detractors, then the episode will repeat itself again and again. *Leopards do not change their spots.*

However, **if someone comes to you and immediately owes up to bad performance or an issue, have the faculty to embrace them**. While there may be some repercussions, they have had the decency to come forward with their hand in the air which is a cry for help. I always listen carefully when someone says, "I screwed up. I know what went wrong and it won't happen again. I'm sorry." I fully realize and accept that fear may be the underlying motive. I remember that I've screwed the pooch many times in my career. If you aren't making mistakes, you aren't trying new things. You aren't pushing the edge of the envelope enough. Mistakes are going to happen. How they are addressed and rectified is the focus.

I'm not alluding to pointing fingers or allocating blame. That's a waste of time. I am espousing that people must give their best efforts day in and day out. They can't go at life in a half-hearted manner. And when things go wrong, we all need to come clean and not make up some half-hearted, lame excuse. "The dog ate my laptop" isn't going to get you very far in life.

Chapter 11 Key:

Put your best effort into doing the job optimally the first time. If you screw up, then admit it and fix it. Ensure that your employees, or team-mates, conduct themselves the same way. Do not accept marginal performance from anyone or that will make you a marginal employee yourself.

Chapter 12

"Minds are like parachutes. They only function when they are open..."

-Sir James Dewar, 1877-1925

The only time you should stop learning and wanting to learn, is when you die. If you aren't learning, you might as well be dead. If you aren't learning, you are deteriorating and devolving. Your mind is the most incredible muscle in your body, and your spirit of curiosity is what powers it. Use them or lose them.

Learning begins with you and your family. I still believe that the majority of the most crucial life lessons that I know were taught to me before I was twelve years old. Don't mistake my meaning that I gave up on learning before I was a teen. On the contrary, my pre-teen learning opened the pathways to my realization that learning would take me to places I had yet to even dream of. **Early in life I realized that my future depended on me adopting a sponge-like approach to knowledge.**

Thinking back to Chapter 1, write down five amazing things you learned before you were thirteen.

1. _____

2. _____

3. _____

4. _____

5. _____

Hopefully, you can think of more than 5 lessons. I just did this exercise myself and had to pull back at 25. Here are 5 lessons I recall, that I think are pretty important for a young kid to know. I haven't stacked my answers to make me look smarter than I was...so don't you.

1. Being small sucked and there are people who will bully you *just because they can.* If you don't have size you'd better figure out how to use your brain and your sense of humor if you don't want to get thumped out every day.

2. There is right and there is wrong. Doing what is wrong can destroy your family's name. Once you lose that, you can't get it back. Pretend your parents are beside you when you are faced with a tricky situation. How would their presence affection your actions?

3. You have a responsibility first to yourself, then your family, your neighbors and your country. My Dad, Uncles and Father-in-law all went off to the war. Post-war, two of them became firefighters who weren't paid very much to risk their lives trying to protect people they didn't even know.

4. Treat others the way you would have them treat your sister.

5. You can succeed at anything if you stick at it long enough and give it your best effort.

Even as a kid, I can remember my mother telling us stories about her upbringing on the farm. Each story had a meaning and if you cared to listen, the meaning would become clear. Mom's stories were always about integrity, being true to yourself and your family, making do with less, and treating others with kindness.

The reason that I asked you to think back to your formative years was to help position what is important to you today. If I asked you to complete a second list of lessons you've learned over the past ten years, can you imagine how different it would be to your "younger" list? I'll wager that most of us would write about our careers, finances, relationships and all those other "grown up" lessons. It's to be expected.

Obviously, we learn different lessons at different stages of our life. What I can expect to be learning in my next twenty years will hopefully be rich and challenging. **What is important in this learning evolution is to not forget what we have learned before**. It's also vital to never think that learning is only for the younger generations. Robert Frost wrote, *"Education is the ability to listen to almost anything without losing your temper or self-confidence."* Education and learning does not mean feeling overly confident that you know it all. No-one knows it all.

Last week, I had lunch with the CEO of a very large corporation which competes globally on a big scale. He shall remain nameless for this story. He's personally worth a fortune and someone I really admire. In his words he told me he was bored and that he'd, "seen it all," in his twenty years as a CEO. In response to my question if he felt that he wasn't learning anymore, he replied a resounding "yes."

"You've seen all then," I echoed skeptically. My own personal career is now 30 years old. I realize that I've only just begun to learn. I've been around the horn a few times, and on many days, feel over-whelmed with paranoia of what's coming my way. Over the years, I've won more than I've lost. But consistently, throughout my career, I have never thought about stopping my own education about business, relationship and life. Sure, a lot of the business issues that arise today, seem familiar. Perhaps I have faced them down in different iterations over the years. But in this current globally explosive and internet-driven environment, everything seems to be shifting at meteoric rates. How my CEO friend was insulated from all this, was beyond me.

"Alright," I began, "let's play a game."

He took a sip from his cup of Expresso and gave me his full attention. "Alright go ahead." I began a story.

"During a recent financial audit of your books, your CFO has been made aware of some questionable discrepancies in your expense reports. This is brought to your attention and you are quite surprised because your personal assistant of twelve years completes your reports. You simply sign them."

"That actually does happen," my friend owed up, setting down his cup. I forged ahead with what his CFO said next.

"Well," your CFO continues, "the discrepancies appear to go back as far as 6 years and I don't know how she managed to slip it through our approvals. Don't have a coronary, but I think this may even go back further."

"How much money are we talking about?" I'm certain you would ask. Your CFO would clear his throat as he replies, "Eighty-four thousand dollars, give or take."

My CEO friend laughed and told me that this was an impossible scenario. He has worked with his assistant for over a decade. She is incredibly talented and loyal to him. In fact, she even does his banking for him.

"Your example is inconceivable. This would never happen," he states firmly, but I see his interest is peaked.

"But as incongruous as this might sound, let's believe for a moment that it has happened," I continue, "and someone inside your company has been having a field day with this information. In fact, in the next few minutes it's going to appear on the internet at the same time that it's e-mailed to your Board of Directors, and home-ward to your wife's computer. Your kids are going to read about this discrepancy on their computers before you see them at the dinner table tonight."

I smiled before continuing. I watched as my friend picked up his spoon and began making circles on the linen table-cloth.

"Your phone is about to ring and your assistant will tell you a reporter from the Wall Street Journal is on hold. He is calling to get you to confirm or deny what they've just read on-line about your financial shenanigans. He's going to ask if you are having an affair with your assistant. In the next 4 hours your CFO is going to receive a phone call from the S.E.C. Your face and name will be in every major newspaper across North America by 5:00 am tomorrow. Every one of your customers will hear about it by lunch. By this time tomorrow your company's stock price will be half of what it is right now. It will still be tobogganing down-hill when the market closes."

I stopped talking and sat back in my chair. I stirred my tea. My lunch mate smiled and cocked his head sideways.

"Okay, you've picked a one in a million scenario that I just can't accept would happen to me."

"Oh, it couldn't happen to you?" I asked smugly. "Tell that to Conrad Black, Kenneth Lay, Jeffery Skilling or Martha Stewart. Share that with James Cayne and Alan Schwartz at Bear Stearns along with all their shareholders who just voted to sell the company for south of 10 bucks," I said, as I picked up my cup of Earl Grey and took a sip.

"It's a completely different world and you can't ever believe that you've seen it all. You haven't. There's stuff coming your way right now that you've never considered, and don't seem prepared to want to learn about. There are employees in your company probably standing two feet on the wrong side of the law. Do you imagine that the CEO of Societe Generale had ever heard of a junior employee named Jerome Kerviel before he (allegedly) forged documents that cost the company almost $7.2 Billion?"

My CEO pal sat up and I could tell he was feeling uncomfortable. No need to press it any further. He had gotten the point. I was sure by this time that I'd given him indigestion. I spoke a little more quietly.

"If you're bored with your current role, then shake it up, or get out and get a new job. Don't sit there comfortably just because you can and the money is good. You've got a long way to go in life and a ton to offer. Don't start going backwards in life just because you think there's nothing more to learn. And don't think that everything around you is in perfect order."

My friend listened very patiently to my last soliloquy and nodded his head. He acquiesced to my point and as the waiter placed our bill on the table, he reached for it. I could tell he was still thinking about my scenario as he pulled out his MasterCard and paid the bill. We parted and I watched him catch a cab back to his office.

A couple of days passed and I picked up a phone message from my friend. He had engaged a consultant in crisis management; had changed all of his pass codes; and, had called a meeting of his executive team to discuss how the company was getting ahead of the internet. He had already spent several hours with his CFO as well as assuming personal control for his, and his wife's banking responsibilities. He signed off the voice mail by saying, "Thanks, you're never too old to learn."

I sit down with all new employees every couple of weeks to welcome them and answer any questions they might have about the company, our clients, or their accountabilities. When they arrive, they each receive a copy of my written job description along with a DVD of me explaining our vision, our company structure, and my expectations of them. At almost every one of these new employee gatherings, I am asked about my reading list and how I became a CEO. I take this opportunity to share with them my perspective on learning. This is what I tell them:

1. **Just because you have graduated from university or college doesn't mean that you stop learning, and wanting to learn.** Aristotle wrote that, *"Education is the best provision for the journey to old age."*

2. Your degree shows a level of persistence, dedication and intelligence. Your education has helped you to learn how to work with other students. It has provided you with a tangible result in a degree for your commitment and in most of your cases, finding the dollars to pay for that degree.

3. **Your schooling has helped you to get this job. It won't keep you here if you don't earn your place.** It was a ticket to ride. Now the real learning and contribution begins. Mark Twain wrote, *"I never let my schooling interfere with my education."* I didn't understand this quote until I had been in the workforce for a number of years and had faced down some pretty hard knocks thrown in my pathway. **Schooling is only the beginning of your true education in life.** The sooner you learn this…the better.

4. Don't depend solely on the company to educate you. Do enroll in all formal training the company offers. Be a sponge in your every day job duties and watch how the seniors make their way to success. Find the best "trainers" in the organization and secure a position under them. Read everything you can about your industry, your company, your competition, your clients and their customers. Inundate yourself with knowledge about the game you've decided to play. **Learn the rules and uncover which are golden and which are "flexible and breakable."**

5. Surround yourself with business colleagues and personal friends of a similar learning mindset. They don't have to be in your industry. In fact, it would be preferable if they weren't.

6. **Keep a journal of your career and write down lessons you are**

learning. When you encounter a problem and find the proper solution, record it for future review.

7. Explore learning beyond your career. Investigate music and the arts. Consider becoming fluent in another language. Mandarin might be a high consideration on that list. Learning another language is like unlocking a different part of your mind and soul.

8. Move beyond your academic mindset of learning. This is now the real world and **the faster you develop solid street smarts, the better your success will be.**

9. As Katharine Hepburn said, *"Become a student of life."* **Don't be so over-whelmed by your career that you don't open your eyes to the world.** Find excuses and financing to travel to places off the beaten path. Pay attention to what we are all doing to this planet. Take on causes that can lead you to think in a variety of different "boxes." Learn something new about yourself every year of your life.

Chapter 12 Key:

Learning is half the fun of life. It's one of the most crucial weapons you have to succeed. When you stop learning, you die a slow boring death.

Chapter 13

"If you are going through hell, keep going…"

-Winston Churchill

When you eat an elephant start at the "right" end. I know you have days where you feel like you are the only hydrant on a street with a thousand dogs. I have days like this on a regular basis no matter how well I plan, or try to anticipate what is coming my way. **Shit happens and you have to prepare yourself for those times when the fan is pointing directly at your face.** Timelines get shortened by your boss. Your kids are sick and your mate is pulling their hair out. The computer eats your project, or you simply weren't smart enough to press the "Save" button often enough. You haven't had a decent sleep in weeks. You can't remember the last time you had sex.

However, when a real work disaster comes flying your way, all the rest doesn't matter. It has to be put aside. Here is the kind of a disaster I'm referring to: Out of the blue, you find yourself dramatically behind the 8-Ball on numerous projects and your world appears to be caving in. Your workload is murderous and you have a migraine that could sink a ship. You are missing timelines left and right, and a major project is due tomorrow that you have let slip. Your boss and co-workers are giving you the evil eye. You're certain that a number of your fellow workers have contributed a few things to submarine your efforts. It all feels so overwhelming that you are parallelized as to where to begin. This is a disaster. So what do you do?

1. *Breathe.* Get somewhere quiet for 5 minutes. Breathe again. Slow down your heartbeat. Adrenalin is one thing. A coronary is another. In *"Don't Sweat the Small Stuff,"* author Richard Carlson wrote, *"Cut yourself some slack. Don't worry about*

being perfect...see your mistakes as learning opportunities."

2. Once you are out of the woods you will do a complete review of "how this managed to happen." Don't start wasting time doing that now. Don't blame or accept blame. **If you are drowning in a lake with a chunk of cement chained to your ankles, you don't start blaming the guy who pushed you out of the boat.** You figure out how pull a Houdini and get to the surface so you can breathe. *You'll get the appropriate revenge, and learning, later.*

3. Write down every issue you are facing in bullet form. Write down the deliverables and timing and why that timing can't be delayed, altered and/or potentially diverted with a quick phone call or e-mail. Typically, one of, or part of, your disasters can be delayed with a very sincere apology and revised due date.

4. **Tackle your issues as you would eat an elephant. There's an old African proverb that says you can't eat this mammoth in one whole bite, but you can if you take bite-sized pieces.** Look at the issues *one at a time as* you would eat the elephant. Bite-sized pieces. Will one to two actions eat up more than one of the bites? Is it possible to cut down this elephant with parallel courses of action?

5. Prioritize the bite-sized pieces into categories like:

   a) If I don't deliver this I will be instantly fired;

   b) If I am late delivering this I will be chastised but not fired;

   c) My boss/client will be so angry with me that this will affect my long-term career with this company...but I won't be fired;

   d) I have a lot of credits built up with this client or boss. Perhaps it's time to cash some of those positive credits; or,

   e) I can risk being late on this specific bite-sized piece for a couple of days.

6. **Make a list of resources and assets you have to help you attack the bite-sized pieces of your elephant.** Include your boss and his/her boss on this list. Call in favors from co-workers. You don't have to go this alone. Do not be afraid to tell your boss or co-workers you are really stuck and need help. Don't waste time

trying to explain how/what/when. Just get them on your team. Be clear on the deliverables and timing. It's better for you to be reprimanded by your boss later, when everything is back in order than later, than when everything is screwed up. The latter might lead to a quick trip to the Exit sign.

7. Ensure your resource teams are all lined up if you are prepping a document/presentation that will need additional help…i.e. preparing a power point; photocopying decks etc.

8. Put your head down, charge that elephant and start eating the pieces one by one.

Chapter 13 Key:

You are going to go through really disastrous times in your life when everything around you is collapsing. The true measure of your character is what you do about it. Remember that when God closes a door, somewhere in the house, He opens a window. Just make sure He knows you're home.

Chapter 14

"You can observe a lot by just watching…"

-Yogi Berra

We all have magical powers to varying degrees. How we understand and use these powers separates us from the pack. Three of these powers are:

1. **Insightful observation**

2. **Active listening**

3. **Verbal communication**

My experience has shown me that people are not using these powers to their fullest. As the hypnotic, magnetic pull of the internet overwhelms us all, mankind is letting go its grasp and ability to use these powers. It's already highly visible in our workplaces, our education system and in our society.

1. **Insightful observation**

Observation is a powerful tool when mastered. How observant are you? Here's a quick test. If you are at home, I need you to tell me everything in the room that's behind you. Close your eyes and don't cheat. What's there? Be very specific. Alright if you are at work, tell me exactly what clothing your boss is wearing today. Tell me what (s)he has on his/her desk. Don't just say *photos*. Describe them as explicitly as you can.

People who observe their surroundings really impress me. Taking in the sights, sounds and smells of the world brings a different perspective and flavor to your life. Why do we tend to do this on vacations 2-3 weeks a year but not for the other 49-50 weeks of the year? Shouldn't this be a daily exercise?

People who observe are able to stop focusing on themselves. That in its own right is a positive action. You can't be in a self-centered state and be properly taking in what is happening around you. It takes a conscious effort to be observant. You are more than just "watching." You are watching and then making conclusions on what you are watching based on your past perceptions and experiences. People who do this well can become astounding prognosticators of what's coming at them in the future. They can uncover opportunities and risks. The Farmers' Almanac is one of the most glaring examples of an institution based using observations to forecast the next years planting and weather cycles. Several years ago I had the good fortune to read from the Almanac which was predicting severe weather the following winter based on their observations of the behavior of certain insects and birds during the spring. It sounded a little far-fetched to me until I heard the same prediction from The Weather Network based on their scientific analysis of the past decade. As it turned out, that particular winter was the worst in 50 years with six major snow and ice storms on top of brutally low temperatures.

I also think people pay more attention to business and economic trends around their careers than they do their own personal lives. Again, it's the case of the shoemaker's children going barefoot. Start being more observant to what is happening in your community and neighborhood. Small events can signal greater outcomes than you might imagine. Look at the behavior of people with more years under their belt than you. Their powers of observation and their ability to gather proper perceptions from what they've witnessed is likely sharper because of longer experience. Some call it "intuition"...I call it "intelligent observation." Same thing.

Unfortunately we now gather our information as it is served up to us. We track down and read blogs and web-sites on the computer.

We read newspapers, watch television programs and go to movies. Why don't we observe the sounds of the earth? Why is it only recently that we have begun to understand carbon foot printing and the reality of how we are damaging our "greater home?" **Get out of your office every day and strive to become more observant of what's happening in the world around you.** Become a student in studying people in the way they are dressed, the way they walk and the way they interact with others. Observe how your customers are interacting with your product. How are you employees or fellow workers acting on the job?

Throughout my career, I have learned more by watching people and observing their actions than I have by reading, or sitting being taught something. You can tell a lot about a person by their posture, the way they "hold themselves," the way they sit, and the way they enter a room. Here's an observation I've made over the years. I can tell how detailed a person is by the state of the soles and heels of their shoes. Are your heels worn down? If the answer is yes, you probably aren't spending enough time paying attention to little details that might be just under the surface. I know we are all busy, but life gets lost by ignoring the little details.

Work on your powers of observation and you'll greatly enhance your interaction with reality. You'll also find it really fun.

2. Power of active listening

Did your mother or father ever use the line, "God gave you two ears and one mouth for a reason?"

I had this particular statement said to me a lot. I'm certain it was used on Mom by her mother and so on. I hear myself telling my children the same thing. They look at me like I'm an idiot. The reason that this saying survives each generation, is because we just don't listen well enough. And when we do listen, a lot of us don't "hear."

When I care to, I have untouchable focus and attention. I can be an absolute laser. I will admit that for the rest of the time, I have the attention span of a half-dead gnat. My mind wanders and I love to day-dream. I often drift off to my favorite movies or books. However, when I am in conversation with someone, this all stops and I turn my attention to them. I owe my total focus to that person out of respect, and genuine interest in what they have to say. I try my best to:

a) look directly into their eyes

b) nod when in agreement

c) use facial expressions to show a question or confusion

d) listen to their exact words and take care to not misinterpret their meaning

e) stick with their flow and not jump ahead to try to prepare my next, or counter statement

f) understand the emotions and intent behind their words

g) hear what is *not being said*

h) feel the truth in their words through their facial expressions and body presentation

There is a lot more to active listening than just blindly accepting the words you are being told. If you study people enough, you'll find trends and consistencies in how particular people interact with you. Some try to blurt out exactly what is on their minds. Others may take a little longer to get to the point. Some never get to the point without a little guidance. Not everyone will be as quick to hear and comprehend as are you. This is where you must decide how much time you are willing to invest in hearing what this individual has on their mind. I still struggle with this element of patience in waiting for people to make their point. Years ago one of my favorite CEOs, Peter Mills told me, "*You don't have to interrupt people to finish what they are trying to say, just because you can figure it faster than they can.*" Imagine this being said with Peter's thick Australian accent, and it comes across sounding more statesman-like.

3. Power of verbal communication

I favor direct conversation that is to the point. I don't like meandering through a conversation. I believe God made candor to be employed liberally. This does not mean being rude or indiscreet. On the contrary, it means preparing your thoughts carefully to cut out any chance of ambiguity. It means anticipating a number of varying responses and being prepared to field them all.

Too many people abuse words. They misuse them, they confuse them, they add in red-herrings which distract and they don't understand the full impact of what they are saying. Discussions with these people are like trying to decipher hieroglyphics.

Winston Churchill remains one of my favorite figures and orators in history. He was a true virtuoso. His documented speeches are works of art with each word carefully selected and each paragraph crafted to bring together a wonderfully clear and visually appealing argument. He wrote:

"If you have an important point to make, don't be subtle or clever. Use a pile driver. Hit the point once. Then come back and hit it again. Then hit it a third time-with a tremendous whack."

How many times have you had a conversation with someone personally, or in a business setting, that when recounted at a later date, is totally different from your recollection? How does this happen? My wife and I will have discussions about previous conversations, and I'd swear that I must be going senile--which I might be, but not in these cases.

A favorite example of mine to make the point of the importance of concise communication took place during the Battle of the Bulge in WWII. Imagine a very cold, wintery and dreary December in 1944. The war had been underway for over 5 years and the soldiers on both sides were bone weary, hungry and wanting to go home. None more than the 101st Airborne, whose dreams of going home would have to wait. The 101st was positioned in Bastogne and had clear orders to hold against the advancing enemy. Within two days, the 101st found itself surrounded, and seriously outnumbered by a superior German force. The outcome of the battle appeared obvious to the Germans. In an effort to avoid a slaughter of the 101st, the German commander respectfully wrote to the American General, demanding an immediate surrender. He stated that it was obvious that the Bastogne defenders could not possibly withstand an assault. They were outmanned, outgunned and out-positioned. His own orders were to attack and take the Bastogne at all costs. Couldn't the American leader see the futility of engaging in a lost cause?

After reading the ultimatum from his counterpart, the commanding officer of the 101st, General Anthony McAuliffe, sent back a well-considered response of his own.

"Nuts," was the one word reply he sent by letter to the German commander. He felt there was nothing more to be said. "Nuts," is all McAuliffe had to say. It communicated his response to the ultimatum along with his sentiment, and his determination. Why elaborate?

General Heinrich von Luttwitz received the one word response with confusion, astonishment and anger. He ordered an immediate assault on the Bastogne. It was a vicious battle and the Germans threw everything they had at the defiant 101st. But the Americans would not give up. The fighting went hand to hand, and the Bastogne defenders held until reinforcements arrived in the form of the 4th Armored Division. Now the winds of war shifted and the German attackers were repelled and defeated.

We can all learn from this example. **Too many times we find ourselves at cross-roads in conversations with our family, friends or business associates because we are not as crystal clear as we think we are being.** We cushion our words in order to not disrupt a situation or hurt feelings. Sometimes we are afraid of provoking an unpleasant or aggressive response.

When it's a personal discussion, we are too focused on selling our own perspective than we are in actively listening to the other person's words. Perhaps we are listening, but not hearing...or not wanting to hear. This is when problems arise. People leave the conversation having heard what they wanted to hear, and not necessarily what was said. Each party goes their separate ways and proceeds according to what they understood to be the outcome of the conversation. It happens all the time. I'll wager you can name 3 quick examples of the last time this has happened to you at work or at home. Go ahead and jot them down:

1._____

–

2._____

–

3._____

–

Here are some touchstones for you to consider in your conversation. First, re-read the quote by Churchill and pay attention to it. Next, decide the two key points you wish to make in a specific conversation. Think how the other person will react to your two points. How will they feel? Is this an "easy" conversation or will it be testy? What might their two key points be? What's the motive behind their thinking? Is there a compromise in where you are both heading?

During any conversation ask questions for clarification. It's alright to play back in your own words what you think you are hearing. I'd encourage you to suggest the other person do the same thing. When you get to the end of the conversation don't just pack up your bags and leave. Summarize what you believe to be the next steps or the agreement that has been made. If it's appropriate, I strongly urge you to immediately send a brief e-mail to the other person thanking them for the conversation, re-stating your position and documenting the agreed-to next steps, timing and accountabilities. None of us can afford to waste time, money or our energies on proceeding in a false direction.

This is not rocket science but much is lost in the translation of conversations when people refuse to understand the importance of the interaction.

Chapter 14 Key:

We have many God-given powers that need to be used every day. Become more observant, learn to listen/hear better and communicate clearly and directly what you mean to say.

Chapter 15

"Golf is a game played on a five-inch course—the distance between your ears..."

-Bobby Jones

Understanding the rules of any game is vital if you hope to win. Understanding the "rules" of how your mind and body work is even more critical. **We all have zones in which our minds, emotions, psyches and bodies operate. Some of these zones are incredibly powerful in helping us to optimize our performance. Other zones are deadly to us. Discovering these "dead zones" is vital to your success.**

You've heard the sports' expression when an athlete is "in the zone." It's that time of the game when an athlete enters a mental, emotional and physical place that (s)he can do nothing wrong. Their concentration is Zen-like; their reflexes are lightning-quick; and, their absolute dominance over their competition is incredible to behold. They appear to be in such peace with the world and have managed to block out anything negative that might hamper their ability to focus on exactly what they are doing. Their ability to "remain in the moment," is continuous and physical pain or fatigue is of no consequence. Victory is only a matter of time.

This euphoric state is being in the zone. Certain athletes seem to be able to move into this stratosphere every time they engage in battle. A red-shirted Tiger Woods on Sunday afternoons. Rafael Nadal's ironman focus when he's playing Roger Federer in a major. The great basketball players like LeBron James, Tony Parker, Kevin Garnett, Kobe Bryant all live in a zone where they shoot the basketball and don't even hang around to see if it went through the hoop. Venus Williams' steel-gazing eyes as she attacks the net for a vicious overhead slam at Wimbledon. Lorena Ochoa's unwavering concentration when she putts for an eagle on the final day of an LPGA tournament. I marvel at Derek Jeter running down a fly ball and selflessly throwing his body into the stands to make the 3rd out. All of these athletes have mentally trained themselves to be able to find their zone at critical points in the game.

Now *for every action there is an equal and opposite reaction* so the opposite negative zones exist for the *same* people. You've seen athletes enter the "dead zone" when they can't buy a hit, score a goal or a sink a basket. Watching them is almost embarrassing. At certain times, no matter how hard they try, or however angry they become, they can do no right. They are in a slump and the fans and press will give them no quarter. The heroes are suddenly "overpaid bums."

These **positive** and **dead** zones exist for all of us in our daily lives, and in our careers. We may not be in a televised arena with millions of people watching our every shift, but we do play in a competitive game every day we leave our homes. People are watching us, and our performance shapes the success of our futures. Astrologers would claim that these zones are simply in the alignment of the stars and planets in juxtaposition with our sun and moon signs. Being your typical Piscean, I must admit a certain understanding and leaning towards these theories. However, my horoscopes are seldom right, so I tend to keep with the theory of the zones.

Firstly, let's clarify how I am using the words "dead zone." Marine biologists have named oxygen-deprived sections of water as "dead zones" because nothing can live or survive in them. I love this term. I relate this term to our lives. **You need to understand times of your day, week, month and year when you are not performing at your best.** Once you discover these periods, you can use them to your advantage. If you fail to recognize these "off times" and continue to make decisions and operate as usual, you are exponentially increasing the probability of erring. I've learned from personal experience that the results of your decisions can improve vastly by understanding, and managing your "dead zones." Let me ask you to think back over the last 3 months and write the answers to these questions. Be honest with yourself.

1. Write down 3 decisions you've made over the past 3 month which generated outstanding results.

   a. _____

   b. _____

   c. _____

2. Write down 3 decisions you've made over the past 3 months that generated weaker results than you had hoped.

   a. _____

   b. _____

   c. _____

3. Write down 3 decisions you've made that within one week you tried to reverse and could not.

   a. _____

   b. _____

   c. _____

Against each of the above think very carefully and write down the exact circumstances under which you made the decisions. Specifically, note down the day and time of day. Is there anything significant about where, or with whom, you made these decisions? Are there any patterns?

Over a decade ago when I first was named CEO, I completed this same exercise over a 6 month period tracking 15 decisions within each category. My findings were consistent and conclusive. Very simply, I made my best decisions on Tuesday/Wednesday/Thursday before 11:00 am, and after 2:00 pm. The weaker results were generated by decisions made early Monday morning or Friday afternoon. The third grouping of decisions which I regretted almost immediately, were grouped in timing around noon every day. With a blinding glimpse of the obvious, I could totally understand the logic behind my zones.

Monday morning I start as slow as molasses in January. It is a combination of action-packed week-ends including my hardest training, and longest distance running day on Sunday mornings. I also have trouble sleeping on Sunday nights that I'm certain dates back to Grade School, when I dreaded going to school on Monday, always fearing that I hadn't completed my homework properly. Friday afternoons fit the bill because I am burned out by the end of the week and my wife and I tend to do our client entertaining on Thursday nights. The real eye-opener was the third category of "regrettable decisions" at noon. I am ruled by my stomach and when I can't see food in front of me on the table exactly at 12:00 noon, I start to panic. In the past, I think I was making decisions out of hunger, and anticipation of wanting to eat. I know this sounds foolish...but is it not more foolish to ignore how you are being affected in your decision making?

Completing this analysis changed the way I made decisions early in my tenure as a CEO. I had motored through almost 18 years of my career not fully understanding my own machine. I hadn't learned my "zones." Take note that the number of decisions you make increases dramatically with your seniority. So learning my "dead zones" as a new CEO helped me to understand when to avoid making any decisions. It took my senior employees approximately one month to get with the program, and I can state without reservation that I dramatically reduced my questionable decisions. For the past decade I can't recall a decision I seriously regret having made. My "batting average" jumped considerably and the outcome of my decisions helped drive the performance of my companies, and my own career.

On a personal note, I also realized that the majority of fusses I had with my wife and kids were taking place first thing in the morning on the drive to work or last thing at night just as we retired to bed. These were two zones for me that just didn't work in having any personal discussions. Sharing this with my wife allowed us to re-orient family discussions to other times of the day. The mornings became more peaceful (less threatening) and my sleep wasn't thrown off by issues being raised just before hitting the sack.

Learning and fully appreciating your "dead zones" is a sure-fire way of improving the results of your decisions at work and at home. Ignoring them will lead to disaster.

> **Chapter 15 Key:**
>
> Uncovering and protecting your "dead zones" is guaranteed to improve your decision making batting average. Ignoring your "dead zones" will hamper your career.

Chapter 16

"I want you to be everything that's you, deep at the centre of your being..."

-Confucius

In helping to spark people to think differently, I often will ask questions that aren't necessarily comfortable. **Sometimes you need to be asked questions that force you to move outside your comfort "zones" to help you to reconsider what you are taking for granted.** These questions apply to anyone at any level of seniority. How would you answer these questions?

1. Are you in the right job? Find something that you can do really well and plays to your strengths. Throughout his entire coaching career, Red Auerbach religiously told his players, *"Just do what you do best."*

2. Do you have a written job description that clearly delineates exactly what you're being paid to do and how your performance will be judged? Do you review that job description on a regular basis and honestly gauge how you are delivering?

3. Have you had a formal written evaluation within the last year? Be prepared to tackle issues you have prior to your evaluation rather than leaving yourself vulnerable to the opening of a Pandora's box.

4. Are you learning something new and interesting about your job, yourself and life every day?

5. Are you being remunerated fairly? How do you know?

6. Is your supervisor someone you can learn from? Not all

supervisors can be stars just like not all coaches deserve to be in the big leagues. When I was growing up and just starting to understand the differences between American and Canadian football, Lou Holtz was the Head Coach of Notre Dame's football team, The Fighting Irish. He had achieved a great deal of notoriety and was at the helm when The Fighting Irish were the college team to beat. Over 27 years as the skipper, Coach Holtz ran up a record of 216-95-7 and was re-known for his ability to get inside his players' heads and help them outperform even themselves. In his book entitled, *"Winning Every Day"*, Coach Holtz outlines a ten point game plan summary he instilled in each player. Here are my eight favorite points:

1. Maintain a positive attitude.
2. Welcome adversity as a learning experience.
3. Act boldly; go for the big play when you are behind.
4. Review your fundamentals; eliminate any short cuts.
5. Think WIN.
6. Adapt to change.
7. Give your best effort at all times.
8. Willingly make the sacrifices that winning demands.

7. **Can you see a career path in the company for whom you work?** Have you discussed that with people who can actually facilitate it for you?

8. Are you continuing to take job interviews elsewhere? It's vital that you keep your finger on the pulse of your industry. Always keep a trap door handy in case something happens in your current position.

9. Are you getting out of your office (or cubicle) and making an effort to meet other people? This is a great way to make alliances with people who might be able to help you achieve greater success. It's also a great method for learning about other areas of the company that you might consider for your next posting.

10. Have you volunteered for over and above projects beyond the call of duty?

11. Do you write down your "to do" list and allocate time against each task? Are your tasks prioritized? If your supervisor tries to add on another job, do you have him/her remove one already on the list?

12. **Are you comfortable in saying "no" to your bosses?** Why not? If you don't learn to say no to a more senior person then your career is going to stall. You will be overburdened with projects and eventually will be spread so thin that your work will slide. You will not shine in your role. People around you, including those who report to you, will lose confidence in your ability to look out for yourself, let alone them.

13. Have you considered working in another city, province, state or country? There is a whole world out there just waiting for you.

14. **Are you bringing new ideas and thinking to the company?** Keep track of your ideas. They might not fly at your current company but that doesn't mean they won't work at your next job. When you have your evaluation, pull out your list of ideas and other accomplishments to make sure your contribution is fairly represented and documented.

15. Most companies will terminate employees the minute sales/ revenue targets are missed. Keep that in mind. **Have a fall-back position ready.** Don't be caught unawares like the deer in the headlights.

16. Get out of the building every day for at least 20 minutes. Go for a walk and get some fresh air. Clear your mind. When you are over-whelmed with the job, go to a museum. That's always an escape that has settled me down when I realize how insignificant I am in the greater scheme of things being displayed in the museum. Chapter 26 will talk about rejuvenating yourself.

17. Network. Network. Network.

18. Become a student of your industry. The company will/can only teach you so much. Know more than your counterparts about your industry, its history and its underpinnings. Read the analysts' reports on your company.

Chapter 16 Key:

Orchestrating and choreographing your career is a career to itself. You must tackle it in complete earnest and stridently attempt to raise yourself above the pack. Most employers will not look out for your best interests. This will be up to you. Be prepared to move outside your comfort "zone."

Chapter 17

"Start with good people, lay out the rules, communicate with your employees, motivate them and reward them. If you do all those things effectively, you can't miss..."

-Lee Iococca

This chapter won't be interesting for every reader. These are questions and considerations I share with people in very senior positions who are running a company. **Often, when people get the corner office, they are so busy and preoccupied with their accountabilities that they don't step back and ask themselves the really important questions.** If you are running an operation or a company, how would you answer these questions and thoughts?

1. You are not doing as great a job as you believe you are. I'm sorry to state this...but it's true. If you care to actually know how well you are doing, hire an outside independent consultant. Have them conduct a totally objective audit of the most senior members of your company (including yourself). *Would you have the courage to have the consultant present the findings back to your entire group without you editing their findings?*

2. Your company is carrying costs of 10-15% that could be cut out. You have too many employees and not everyone knows what you expect them to be doing.

3. You are losing revenue/sales because of the way your employees are interacting with current and would-be customers.

4. Do you have replacements standing on the sidelines for your 15 most critical employees? Have you identified your own replacement?

5. You have an employee on staff you think should be fired. Why are you failing to take that action to have the employee terminated? Other employees recognize this person's shortcomings and are questioning your judgment/commitment, for delaying to act. Your job is to ensure you have the right people in the right places at the right time. If someone needs to be removed then remove them logically, justly and promptly.

6. Are you being fairly remunerated? Just because you are a CEO doesn't mean you can't be asking for a raise that fits the contribution you are making to the company. However, don't ask unless: a) you believe it is warranted; and, b) you are prepared to leave within a reasonable timeframe if they refuse without an acceptable counter-offer.

7. Your customers' needs and your competitive framework are morphing more often than you change the oil in your car. It's virtually impossible to know what is coming your way in the next six months, let alone the next two years. As the CEO, you can rest comfortably behind the solid product offerings and current financial stability of your firm. You can believe your company can "weather any storm." Or **if you want to be a true leader, begin to re-build your operations and talent resources to be able to give you the flexibility to "course correct" regardless of the market shifts coming your way**. The longer you wait to build this flexibility into your thinking and operations...the greater your risk of failure. Jeff Bezos, CEO Amazon told Josh Quittner in a *Fortune Magazine* interview, *"The trick is to position the company so even in a wide variety of scenarios you can pursue more fundamental things."*

And along this same theme, James F. Moore wrote in *"The Death of Competition"* that:

"The traditional industry boundaries that we've all taken for granted throughout our careers are blurring-and in many cases, crumbling."

8. How many job interviews have you taken lately? As I wrote in the last chapter it is imperative that you don't leave yourself "un-networked." Over the past two years, I know six Presidents who have found themselves on the wrong side of a termination discussion. To varying degrees, the six are all strong contenders, and to a person, have proven themselves "under fire." Tenure-wise, they are all within three years of each other and were not terminated because of weak performance.

In very short order, three of the six found new positions that suited their needs and seniority perfectly. During the time it took for them to secure their new positions they did not face any personal financial, family or emotional issues. Their networks stepped up to the plate and helped them land safely. In one case, one of those three Presidents had a job lined up before his last day on the previous job. The remaining three ex-Presidents are still on the street diligently hunting for new jobs. What do these latter three share in common? Firstly, **they didn't build a network of contacts or potential future employers**. Secondly, they limited their "reach" beyond the confines of their current employment. **They also didn't protect their *own brand*.**"

In the book, "*CEO Capital*," author Leslie Gaines-Ross discusses the importance of CEO's paying attention to their personal reputations and the fact that they are under a magnifying glass every day they are on the job. *"CEOs earn credibility by being consistently truthful and delivering on their promises. They also earn it by matching behavior with the values they espouse."* It's far too easy for leaders to be so focused on the tasks at hand that they are not looking to their own careers and developing plans and strategies for their eventual exit.

Here's a drill for you that should take no more than ten minutes. It's time to role-play. You've just been given a head's up that due to a company restructuring your position is going to be terminated. This is not something you can avoid. It's a fact. Given your strong performance, the company is going to offer you a senior position overseas. In other times in your life, this might suit you perfectly. Unfortunately due to family constraints and needs, you can't make this work. Given your contract, you will be given a fair severance package and a strong endorsement. On the chart below prioritize a list of contacts you can <u>doubtlessly</u> count on to either:

a) offer you a new job;

b) introduce you to a potential employer; or,

c) provide you with a stellar character and business reference.

Your list should have no less than 15 names on it, most of which should fall into the second category. If you've protected your career properly you have at least 2 names in the first category.

Contact Name	Title	Phone/E-mail	How they can help me
1.			
2.			
3.			
4.			
5.			
6.			
7.			
8.			
9.			
10.			
11.			
12.			
13.			
14.			
15.			

Look over your list. How well have you connected yourself to people who can help you if things were to go sour in your current job? I fervently believe that when God closes a door, He opens a window. Why not make it a little easier for Him by making sure your house has a lot of windows from which to choose? It's also quite important that this be a two-way street. You must help people who come to you when things go wrong in their career. This is like a game of "pay forward." I've helped a lot of peers, friends, clients and friends of friends get into new positions. Sometimes I've given character references and sometimes I've simply forwarded a resume by e-mail. Don't shut your door when someone comes calling for help. I'm not saying you have to spend 30% of your life relocating people you know. I am saying that someone you help today, may be the person who helps you tomorrow.

9. Do you know the name of the person who delivers your mail? Do you say hello to everyone in the elevator or in the hallway. Being greeted by the CEO is like getting a bonus. I still have notes sent to me by my CEOs throughout my 30 year career. The notes and letters meant a lot to me. To everyone you encounter in your company, why not say a sincere, "Hello. How are you?"

10. How many new ideas are being brought to you weekly? Do you encourage new thinking and ideas? We all immediately answer "yes" but exactly how are you doing that? Do you monetarily reward people for new ideas? Is your company structured for new ideas to be implemented? Do you have a procedure for evaluating new ideas? Tim Penner is the President of P+G Canada and he recently asked a group of senior marketers at a conference I was chairing, *"Are you set up to discover unexpected solutions?"* Quickly jot down the names of your five most senior leaders in the company. Beside each name, write down one "big idea" they've brought to your table in the last six months. Don't be surprised if your chart has a few blanks.

Top five leaders	Ideas brought forward in last 6 months
1._____	_____
2._____	_____
3._____	_____
4._____	_____
5. _____	_____

11. Is your company a positive vehicle for enhancing your community and country? How much of your time and your company's time are you allocating to help a good cause? Can you be donating company product? I know that requests come at you from all directions but why not earmark three charities each year, and solicit help from your employees to help make a difference. Not only will you help others in need, you'll build your firm's reputation on the street. This attitude will make your firm a more desirable place to work, or perhaps do business with. It also sends your employees a message of the character of the President for whom they work.

12. Would you consider yourself a "teaching" President? If the answer is no then you are missing out on a critical function for your employees... especially your most senior ranks.

13. Do you share your vision, credos, successes and failures with your employees? Do you give your employees a "reason to believe and be optimistic?" Napoleon said, *"A leader is a dealer in hope."* Would your people consider you to be incorruptible? Are they correct in this perspective?

14. Do you spend more than 15% of your time sitting at your desk? If the answer is yes...then STOP DOING THAT. The results of your *hiding* in your office will be cataclysmic to your company.

15. Here's a question I know most of you struggle with. **How do you balance the current DNA and history of your company with the need for change to keep ahead of your competition?** It's the age old clash of

heritage versus innovation. *"Fortune Magazine's"* Richard Siklos posed this question to Bob Iger, the CEO of Disney who responded, *"I'm a big believer in respect for heritage, but I'm also a big believer in the need to innovate and the need to balance that respect for heritage with a need to be relevant."*

16. Never under-estimate the power your title and position holds over people in your company. Would they respect you as a person, laugh at your jokes or be your friend if you weren't their boss? Interesting question, isn't it? Don't ever fool yourself with your answer.

Nelson Mandela just celebrated his 90th birthday. He was interviewed by Richard Stengel for an enlightening article in *"Time Magazine."* He spoke of his *"8 Lessons of Leadership."*

1. Courage is not the absence of fear—it is inspiring others to move beyond it.

2. Lead from the front--but don't leave your base behind you.

3. Lead from the back—and let others believe they are in front.

4. Know your enemy—and learn about his favorite sport.

5. Keep your friends close—and your rivals closer.

6. Appearances matter—and remember to smile.

7. Nothing is black or white.

8. Quitting is leading too—knowing how to abandon a failed idea, task or relationship is the most difficult decision a leader has to make.

Chapter 17 Key:

Don't become a leader just to get the corner office and money. Become a leader because you want to do great things. Become a leader when you've learned that you are nothing without your people. Become a leader when you put others before you. Become a leader when you have learned where to lead. Being a leader does not mean giving up your accountability to look after your own career.

Chapter 18

"Integrity has no need of rules…"

-Albert Camus

Your integrity is the undeniable core of who you are. You must never fall prey to, "I was told to do it so I did" mentality. If something seems odd or wrong then DON'T DO IT, no matter who is instructing you to do it. My rule of thumb when I'm faced with making a really ugly decision is to pretend that my mother is sitting in a chair beside me. I think about what my decision will be and if I could turn and face my mother and get a smile. If I can't foresee that smile then I know there is something wrong with my decision. I also try to take my decision back to the simplest, and most basic of its foundations. I ask if there is truth and justice in the decision I am making.

"Always tell the truth," said Mark Twain, *"that way you won't have to remember what you said."*

Throughout my upbringing, my parents impressed upon me the importance of your "family's name." It's not just a name that you own. It's shared by every relative and the positive or negative actions of one relative affect the entire clan's reputation and credibility. Based on my experience, it's really very hard to "win back" your reputation and credibility once a nail has been hammered into your family's name. Re-earning the trust of others is almost damned impossible. Frankly, even regaining the trust you have in yourself won't come easy. Oliver Wendell Holmes wrote, *"What lies behind you, and what lies ahead of you is of very little importance when it is compared with what lies within you."*

Something that I've witnessed time and again bothers me greatly. I've learned that in general, people enjoy watching others be knocked down in life. The circumstances often don't matter. They look for others to fall from the pedestal upon which they've been placed…by the same people looking for them to fall. Take care that you don't join the mob awaiting someone else's failure and fall off the pedestal. Also take care about getting up onto any pedestals yourself.

As you move through your career, it becomes readily apparent that your reputation takes years of consistency to be built. **Don't believe for a second that once you've built your reputation it is unimpeachable. A reputation that took years to build can crumble in only seconds.** Read the financial pages and the list of CEOs who are sitting behind bars weren't raised to be criminals. I can name a half a dozen "A" list actors who have destroyed their careers by saying the wrong thing in front of a camera. Remember to think before you act. No one is immune to having their reputation and their core integrity put before the flame.

Oh yes, a cautionary word on Facebook, MySpace.com, FlickR and the rest of the Internet. To all you moronic teenagers who are posting photos of yourselves in various stages of undress, drinking bottles of whiskey and smoking dope. Think how this reflects on your parents and your family. What does this say about them? Think a few years down the road when you are applying for a job. How unfair will it be when your interviewer receives an e-mail from the person against whom you are competing for the job? Let's say this e-mail is a download of you partying, drinking it up and acting like an imbecile. What does that say for your maturity, professionalism and your integrity? Forget what it says about the backstabber who slagged you by sending the e-mail. That's irrelevant. The net of it is, your chances at getting the job have just been compromised.

You ability to maintain your integrity will be greatly enhanced if you are courageous and diligent in protecting your absolute core.

When I was in my early twenties, my older brother Bill recommended that I read Carl Von Clausewitz's *"On War."* Not the easiest read in the world. It seemed to have more forwards and introductions than any other ten books I had read up to that date. *"On War"* has served as a mini-bible to many great military leaders over the past two centuries. Von Clausewitz wrote:

"Courage is of two kinds: first, physical courage, or courage in presence of danger to the person; and next, moral courage, or courage

before responsibility, whether it be before the judgment-seat of external authority, or the inner power, the conscience."

Chapter 18 Key:

Integrity is the glue that holds your character in place and you must never breach it.   It will be the core to everything successful you ever achieve. Protect it with your life.

Chapter 19

"You have to believe in yourself…"

-Sun Tzu

Getting fired early in my career was the exact kick in the teeth I needed. I'll leave out the sordid details but I caught a bullet behind the left ear in my late 20s. In hindsight, I took a job that I should never have taken. I ignored my mentors' advice and in my arrogance thought that "I knew better." I had been rocketing through my career and got easily swayed by the offer of a big title, and what at the time, seemed to be an incredible bump in my salary. I was offered a company car and a good number of people to supervise. The company had a blue-chip reputation and was known for its aggressive and no-prisoners approach to business.

I just didn't do my homework on the new opportunity, or I would have discovered that the company's basic philosophies, working ethics and "personality" were in complete contradiction to my own. How easy it would have been for me to talk to some ex-employees and headhunters (aside from the one selling me on the company) about what I was considering. The people who knew my personality and working style knew that I was not a fit for the company. They told me and I ignored them. A proper analysis would have shown that moving to this organization was 100% counter-intuitive. Unfortunately for me at the time, I discovered all of this after I had accepted the new job…but <u>before</u> my first day of work was over. At 9:00 pm on my very first day, I was still sitting at my desk with a load of work. I looked out to the sparkling lights of the city and thought to myself:

"What in God's name have I done?"

I can honestly say that I was miserable at that job every subsequent day going forward. I dreaded getting up in the morning, and my nights were a sleepless frustration. I invested ridiculous hours trying to make it work out, but the harder I tried, the more frustrating it became. Soon, I knew that the whole gig wasn't going well. I felt like an idiot most of the time...always on the outside of the "in" performers. I was a problem for them. They knew it, and so did I. Each passing week was drudgery and ridiculous hours. I actually calculated that I was making less money per hour than I had earned making minimum wage during my last summer job in high-school. My non-work time was spent worrying about the job. **I felt paralyzed and for the first time in my career, I didn't know what to do.** My pride prevented me from discussing any of this with my mentors...in particular, the ones who had advised against taking the job. The strain I felt every day began to take its physical toll on me. I couldn't sleep. My appetite waned. I didn't have any energy to exercise. I was in a personal relationship that went sour mainly because my mind was in a really bad place. My spirit was having its teeth kicked in every day. My work output began to suffer and if there was a way of making an error on the job, I made it. Have you figured out that once you find yourself on a bad streak...it's really hard to get back on track?

Even my co-workers were completely aware of the strain and the difficulty. No one offered help or guidance. Not one person stepped up to the plate for me. This was all about job competition and I was the wounded zebra with a pack of lions surrounding me in the Savannah. It was youth, or naivety that stalled me from taking matters into my own hands, because looking back at that situation today, I would not have sat there waiting for something to happen. Boy, if I had only known then what I know today.

Finally, I caught a bullet and was terminated. Although it seemed like an eternity before it happened, it was actually before my first year was completed. I received a totally fair severance on the way out the door. The company conducted themselves very professionally. I was told, off the record, that I was a bad fit--a round peg in a square hole...or a square peg in a round hole. Either way, as pegs go...I wasn't the right shape for them.

With the firing came the opportunity for me to step off the treadmill I had been running on, like a cocaine-addicted hamster. **In the first few months that followed, I remember being extremely embarrassed and ashamed. I felt everyone would look at me like I was**

a failure. I didn't even own up the full truth to my parents, and told them I had left the company. They found this odd given that I didn't have a new job lined up to step into.

I was convinced my future prospects had just been cut short and my career was in the dumper. After all, I had been visibly rejected from a blue chip marketing organization. I was the wrong-shaped peg! However, after the first few months of my personally-imposed shame passed by, I began to gather my thoughts about the entire exercise. I considered the mistakes and my role in the termination. I had not researched the depth of the waters and had decided to dive in head first. I also hadn't really understood the true mechanics of the kind of environment, leadership approaches and interpersonal needs that I personally had to have, in order for me to be my best. This all gave me considerable pause for thought. I needed to get away from everything. So that's what I did. I took some time to travel, saw some friends, and cleared the bleeding cobwebs from my head. I determined that I could either retreat to wallow in self-pity or I could use this kick in the teeth to my advantage. Eleanor Roosevelt wrote that, *"No one can make you feel inferior without your consent."* What a wonderful statement. **No one can make you feel inferior without your consent**. I decided not to let my former employer make me feel inferior. Regardless of the pressure I was putting on myself, I would not give that consent. I also began considering that perhaps I wasn't the wrong-shaped peg. Perhaps they were the wrong-shaped hole for me.

Seeking a new job right away didn't seem logical until I got all my ducks in a row. I sat down and wrote out a thorough analysis of myself (see Chapter 1). This inner-review was much more honest than I had ever completed before. **We have a tendency of sugar-coating feedback, even when it's to ourselves: Especially when it's to ourselves**. I removed any coatings and delivered myself the most candid review I could muster. I realized with the analysis staring me in the face, that there was no way I could have been successful in that job. I had been doomed to failure before I showed up on the first day of work. Looking at my analysis, I started to understand what I needed to succeed. I saw the landmines that would explode underfoot every time I entered non-friendly territories. It was so obvious and the next steps appeared to be crystal clear. I ranked the fifteen most important factors for me to be successful. I compared and prioritized a variety of industries against those factors, and then narrowed down a list of companies that fit the bill. It wasn't an easy process but it was proactive, logical and exactly what I needed to do. I was no longer contrite about being fired. The act itself became a catalyst for me to rethink my entire life's game-plan.

With a termination you will go through a plethora of feelings and anxieties. No one likes to be rejected, especially publically. Even when an employee hates the job, they still want to be the one to decide when to leave. The severance package helps but it doesn't remove the sting of public embarrassment. Here are some things to consider if a bullet hits you on the back of your head and you find yourself being fired:

1. **Don't react in anger or surprise.** This has already been discussed and the paperwork has been signed. They have decided you are gone. Know when to accept reality.

2. **Don't argue or ask for reasons.** The company does not legally have to say a thing. Understand that your brain won't be operating on all cylinders. You won't be hearing properly during the meeting anyway. Sit quietly and even if you knew "something was up" keep your counsel to yourself. Anything you say can be brought up at a later date. You can ask how this is being communicated internally, to clients and suppliers.

3. Don't cry. This is a business meeting. Tough it out.

4. The company should have something in writing to give you. Ask for it if they don't. **Don't sign anything until you see a good lawyer.**

5. The company may request that you to leave immediately, and that's probably best. Under certain circumstances they may ask you to finish up a project over a couple of weeks. I'm not certain I would agree to do that, but I wouldn't decide until I had been advised by my lawyer.

6. If you are requested to leave immediately, then do so. Leave any personal belongings in your office. Turn over any company property: cell phone, Blackberry, credit cards, door pass cards and keys. Ask for a written receipt.

7. Call a friend or a family member. Do not try to shield this from your significant other. This is not a time for secrets. **Try not to be alone.**

8. If anyone from the company calls you after the firing, don't

discuss anything. Tell "well-meaning" workmates that you will talk to them in a few days. Thank them for their call but do not discuss the firing under any circumstances.

9. **See a lawyer immediately.** Take all documents with you including the dismissal letter, your original job offer letter, your job description, any evaluations, any letters from your boss/clients/co-workers and a paycheck to show your financial history. Don't let your lawyers pump you up with expectations of ridiculous amounts of severance. It should be an attitude of fair play that will tide you over until you find a new job. It should be within the laws set out to protect employees.

After you have signed the paperwork, see if you can arrange to meet with your supervisor for a coffee and a candid conversation. Don't go in with a bad attitude. Try to learn more about the termination. What could have been done to avoid it? Where did you go off the rails? What were the warning signs that you missed? Be gracious and polite. Don't argue or try to defend your performance. That's like trying to pinch an angry rhinoceros when his foot is crushing your head. Move on. Display the true content of your character. Your career is not a one trick pony and you will have many jobs before you are done. James A. Michener wrote, *"Character consists of what you do on your third and fourth tries."*

Now here's the best advice you are going to get. You've just been terminated. You have the cheque in hand. Your benefits and health coverage are in order. Do not rush out to any interviews until you clear your head and complete the analysis in Chapter 1. Here's what you are going to do instead.

Have some fun! **You've just been given a free "get out of jail" card and a paid leave of absence.**

Use every minute of every day of your "hiatus" to exercise your brain. Play some golf. Take a holiday. Travel across the country. Go to Australia. Stay up late and watch movies you haven't seen in years. Go home and visit Mom and Dad. Change your diet. Don't drink too much but do the things that bring you the most pleasure in life. Before you know it, you are going to be in a new job that you'll probably enjoy better than your last one. You'll look back at your "working hiatus" and you should smile with what you learned about yourself, and the wonderful way that you used that time to make yourself healthier, smarter and wiser.

I fervently believe that everyone should be fired at least once in their career: Preferably not because of incompetence or legal cause. In life, we all need a setback like a well-placed kick in the groin that takes you down to one knee and sucks the breath right out of you. Whether you collapse on the ground in a cadaverous state or, you catch your breath and get up ready to fight, are the true test of your mettle. People around you are watching how you conduct yourself after you've been hit. Show the world the true rich content of your character. Keep your counsel to yourself and be professional at all times. **If you have nothing positive to say about the company that nailed you, then don't say anything at all.** Use this kick in the groin to learn and make yourself stronger.

If I had not been fired I would never have changed industries and this would have been a major mistake for my personality and skill set. I would have likely ended up in a mid-level job in a large corporation, or perhaps in the President's role in a much smaller company. I wouldn't have been "forced" to re-evaluate my entire game-plan top to bottom. I would never have had to "take a knee" and decide for myself whether to crumble in self-pity, or get back into the game. Doing the latter paid off in spades and was the biggest confidence booster you can imagine.

Years ago I read the speech that Steve Jobs of Apple gave as a commencement address to the 2005 Graduating Class at Stanford. Steve Jobs is one of my favorite CEOs. His speech was very emotional and telling. You can pull it up on the Internet. If you've been fired in your career, I strongly suggest you read this because it encapsulates everything I'm trying to say in this chapter. We all know how successful Steve Jobs and Apple are today: Just pick up your I-Pod and hit some tunes. But you may not know that it hasn't always been a bed of roses for him at Apple. Allow me to share a few of his key statements from the address:

"We had just released our finest creation—the Macintosh—a year earlier, and I had just turned 30. And then I got fired. How can you get fired from a company you started?...so at 30 I was out. And very publicly out. What had been the focus of my entire adult life was gone, and it was devastating. I really didn't know what to do for a few months... I was a public failure and thought about running away from the (silicon) valley. But something slowly began to dawn on me that I still loved what I did. I had been rejected, but I was still in love. And so I decided to start over. I didn't see it then, but it turned out that getting fired from Apple

was the best thing that could have ever happened to me. It freed me to enter one of the most creative periods of my life."

In my heart of hearts, like Steve Jobs, I look back on being fired as having had a profound and positive effect on the launching of my real potential in my career and in my life. And for that, I sincerely and respectfully thank the bastards who did it. Amen.

Chapter 19 Key:

Recognize that the odds are high that you are going to get fired, at some point in your career. When it happens, make sure you get the true reasons. Don't buckle. Get a good lawyer. Catch your breath and when you are ready, head back in for Round Two. It's no big deal.

Chapter 20

"Home is where one starts from…"

-T.S. Eliot

How Green Was My Valley. This is the name of one of my favorite books, written by Richard Llewellyn. John Ford produced the book into the 1942 Academy Award winning movie starring Walter Pigeon, a very young Roddy MacDowell, and a magnificently beautiful Maureen O'Hara. *"How Green Was My Valley,"* is the touching story of a community's involvement in Welsh coal mining town…circa 1900. The narrator was raised as a child in that village, and tells of his family's struggles during a miners' union strike. With little prospects for the future, his older brothers leave to find their fortunes in America. The thirteen year-old lad watches the breaking apart of his family. He recounts his parent's attempts to protect the family and traditions they hold dear. His life is filled with love and he is an unusually bright young boy. When he is sent out of the valley to attend a city school, he encounters physical bullying from the other school children, all of whom are from wealthier families: Families who have never had coal dust on their clothing. With some intervention from his family, he endures and overcomes the issues at school. The miners' strike takes a terrible toll on his family and the community. He survives working in the mine and, in mid-life, looks back at his childhood and realizes how wonderful and rich his life had been, in that coal-mining valley. He remembers the kindness of his family and neighbors, and how despite it all, they managed to find their way through.

This story holds a particularly special place for me. I wasn't raised in a coal mining town but I was brought up in an idyllic environment in small town Ontario. You knew your neighbors and your friends. There were decent schools and a hospital. The outdoor surroundings were rich with parks, farms, rivers, beaches, fishing and hunting. People were kind and approachable. I had a house I loved to come home to with a mother who would love you without fail or reservations. Her compassion and love was as infectious as was the sense of right and wrong that she instilled in us all. My father was a fireman for most of his adult life after he got released from a P.O.W. camp in Germany in WWII. He was a larger than life person for me growing up and now in his 80s, is someone I admire and hold dearly. My family life was pretty amazing...I just didn't know how amazing until many years later.

I had a real lesson in humility when I left home in my late teens. I arrived at university bright-eyed and very naïve. To that point in my life, I had little "big city" experience. When I pulled into the residence where I would be living, I discovered that the majority of the other students had really amazing clothes and most importantly, their own cars. Now, these weren't ten year-old wrecks that they had scrimped and saved to purchase. On the contrary, they were new, shiny and very expensive.

"I got that for graduating in the top half of my class in high school," Jeff shared with the group. He was referring to the cherry red '78 Ford Mustang sitting across the street.

"It's only got 300 miles on it."

Top half of the class got him a Ford Mustang. I mused what would vehicle Jeff would have been given by his parents for being in the top quartile? Others seated at the table piped up with similar stories about their new cars or vacations they had just returned from. I sat quietly at the end of the table feeling like a Puritan. After hearing about everyone's car, I listened to how everyone had travelled over the summer. It never occurred to me that students didn't work every summer to save money for university tuition, books and living costs. Of the eight or nine young men at the table, only three of us had worked the previous summer. Two of the employed kids had worked in their fathers' companies.

"What did you do this summer Breen?" asked one of the boys whose appearance looked like he should have been modeling for GQ.

"You have any trips worth talking about?"

I had *no trips worth talking about* and had worked every summer in order to fund my university education. I didn't have a car, nor did I have any expectations of having one. My parents had worked damned hard to give us a really decent upbringing and they had sacrificed much for us. Not something you could be ungracious about. I shared with the group that I had worked for the phone company installing telephone cables. If I was lucky, I might get hired back on for each summer throughout my university. That was it for me!

My table mates weren't rude about it, but I realized then and there that I was different...the odd duck. I couldn't keep up with stories from my private school because I hadn't gone to a private school. I couldn't talk about my dad's company because my dad didn't have a company. Being the odd duck wasn't a comfortable feeling and it was only going to get worse.

As the school year unfolded, I felt like a country bumpkin. It was evident that I was so out-classed by the other students in the residence that I learned to keep to myself. They did everything I didn't. They golfed at private golf clubs. I had never golfed. They skied in Aspen. I had skied once and one of the people with me broke her leg. They had tailored suits and wonderful clothes, and I had two pairs of jeans, one pair or cords, sneakers, and one pair of dress shoes. They spoke of holidays in France and California, and fathers who were written up in the business sections of the newspapers. I had never even been on a plane. One of the hardest things I had to work through was watching my residence floor mates skip classes and meals only to order in food late at night. I wouldn't miss a class or meal that I had already paid for. I just couldn't understand their attitude and behavior. I had calculated to the dollar the cost of every meal and class. Wasting this money seemed criminal to me...even if they were doing it on "daddy's ticket."

As the four years of university progressed, I developed a real chip on my shoulder. I also fostered a bit of disdain for the students who seemed to have it all and took it for granted. I knew this was immature and judgmental but their behavior really bothered me. I couldn't get over the money that the other students seemed to have access to. I was struggling to make ends meet and working like a dog.

It didn't change post-university when I entered the working world. This lesson of "haves and have nots" continued to stare me in the face when I met my new co-workers. As in university, a good number seemed to have come from families with a ton of dough. Most of my peers spoke of private schools, summer homes and Christmas vacations in Colorado. Boy, I really felt out of place. With each passing month and year, the chip on my shoulder grew heavier.

Looking back now, I am ashamed to admit that for a number of years, I regretted my small town upbringing and the circumstances of my lower-middle class family. What a waste of energy and thinking that all was. How childish. Thank goodness that the progression of time allows for a little maturity to set in. **Time and experience have an uncanny ability to change how you see things in life.** With the passage of my career, I watched closely as the careers of more privileged competitors fell by the way-side. As I got to know them better, our conversations took on a more serious nature. My earlier impressions had not been well-founded. I heard uncomfortable stories about their upbringings and lack of parental involvement, or love. I discovered that they may have had money and private clubs but a good number had parents that they really didn't know: Parents who had not made time for them, as my parents had for me. To my amazement, I learned that a number of them had actually been envying me and my upbringing. Can you imagine my surprise at hearing that? What a revelation. The barriers I had erected over the years slowly began to erode. I started to rethink my upbringing, and it finally dawned on me that I was exactly who I had been raised to be. I couldn't pretend to be otherwise. My upbringing was pretty decent when you put it squarely on the table.

I was the son of a very brave man who had spent his adult life fighting for his country during the war, and then for his community as a Fire Chief. I was the son of an incredible woman who had more spirit, love and earthly-intelligence than anyone I had met in my own adult life. I had been reared to know right and wrong. I had been taught by the daily example of my parents and siblings how to conduct myself. As I rethought my youth, I remembered the laughter, the card games, the Christmases, the stories and rooms full of relatives. I remembered sitting out on our front porch watching the world unfold on our very street and playgrounds. How had this escaped me for so long? I felt foolish for not having seen the reality of what was really important in life. Why I had been so threatened by fancy cars and material possessions seemed now to have been so foolish and such a waste of time and energy. Comparing my life and circumstances to other students, co-workers or neighbors had been totally inane.

It took time but I found peace in my own skin. In fact, it took years, but with the arrival of wisdom, I finally realized how green my valley truly was, and had been forever. I had had it made and didn't even know it.

Was your valley green? Is it now?

Chapter 20 Key:

Remember from whence you came, and never be ashamed of your beginnings. There is a reason you came from there. Acknowledge that, and find the good in it.

Chapter 21

"I never did anything alone, whatever was accomplished was accomplished collectively…"

-Golda Meir, 1977

You can tell a lot about a person by the people with whom they surround themselves. My Mother always said she could tell how good a kid was by the company of friends (s)he was surrounded with. I learned that she right, and this insight helped me to gain a better understanding of people. Even now, I incorporate this adage into how I interview candidates for positions in my company. I always ask this same question mid-way through the interview.

"Describe your best friend for me."

The reaction to the question is almost as important as the answer itself. It is a rather intrusive question but my job is to find out if the interviewee is a good fit. If I see an automatic smile and the person shifts in their seat, then this change in *demeanor* indicates I'm about to hear a really good story. From the *words selected* in the answer, I'm going to hear explicitly what the interviewee holds as being important in life. I also pay great attention to the *inflection* of the words. Here's a sample response.

"My best friend is incredible and I've known her for years. (*said with a wide smile and a shifting in the chair*) We've had ups and downs in our relationship but she's always there when I need her. She's smart as a whip but never makes other people feel stupid. (*another smile and then a reflective look*) Kathy has a real sense of character and strong morals. Her spirit to help others is indefatigable. Her family is like my own and even in her teen years she kept very close to her folks. She works in

Chicago and loves her job. She puts a lot of effort into it. I just love her and think the world of her." *(interviewee speaks this quieter and then looks off, thinking of her friend)*

An answer like this sample response is exactly what I want to hear...and how I want to hear it. By discussing her best friend, the interviewee has shared with me what attributes she holds to be her "truths" in life: sense of character/strong morals/spirtit/family/loyalty/ love. It's what she admires about people and personality traits she strives to possess. If she is being genuine with her words, her response will be delivered in a relaxed manner with a big smile. Her eyes will brighten and possibly dance a little. The interviewee will likely sit back and slow down her speech. With this very simple question, the interviewee will let down their guard for moment and simply become someone's best friend. The transparency resulting from my question allows a window to open for me to look inside...if just for a moment. This is not something that can be practiced and well-rehearsed. People don't lie about their best friends.

I've had such an array of answers to this specific question about describing your best friend. I've heard responses about best friends who are crazy, always calling in sick for work, party animals, and friends who are never around when you need them. It is incredible how the interviewee responding along this line, will become agitated with their response, which also sends me a variety of mixed signals. *"If this friend is such an incredible problem in your life, then why are you putting up with it?"* I can't help but believe that the interviewee's personality is analogous to the person they are describing.

Why else is this question so revealing and pertinent? **The people you spend time with are people who influence you, teach you and affect your moods.** They can bring peace and optimism to your life, or they can be a real anchor around your neck. They can fulfill a needed role of motivating you to greater success or they can be a drain that brings you down. **You need to be very careful with whom you surround yourself.** Your friends and business acquaintances should all be bringing new thinking to your table. They should challenge your opinions and philosophies. With them, you should be investigating world events and how all your futures are going to unfold. Sometimes your friends are people with whom you can just hang out: No talk necessary and no expectations. Your selection of friends should include diversity of ethnicity, backgrounds and skill-sets. If you are a lawyer, don't surround yourself with other lawyers. You want people with different mindsets, histories and perspectives helping you to broaden your own. You want a rich cross-fertilization of thinking and ideas surrounding you *every* day.

Write down an exhausted list of everyone you know. Leave off your family members or business associates. There may be people you put on this list who are not quite in the friend category but people you might want to have as a friend. You may add on names of people who were friends but you've lost track of. I want you to think about your relationship with each person on the list. This is a two-part exercise. **First**, take a read of the statements outlined below. These are attributes and factors that I feel are important for my friends to possess. I'm sure a lot of them will apply to you--some may not. **Secondly,** before answering/ranking the statements, I would like you to prioritize them in importance in how you look at your friendships. On the LEFT side of each statement place an A, B or C priority ranking. Once you have the prioritization of importance in place make ten copies. Then go back and answer/rank the statements for each friend as follows:

1-2 Totally disagree

3-4 Disagree somewhat

5-6 Agree with qualifiers

7-8 Agree most of the time

9-10 Totally agree

(friend's name:):

<u>A/B/C Priority</u>   <u>1-10</u>

___-makes me feel good about myself   ____

___-challenges me to think about things   ____

___-would be there if I were in need   ____

___-never makes me feel I'm on their "B" list   ____

___-makes me laugh, and laughs at my jokes   ____

____-is someone I admire and respect   ____

____-doesn't make me feel bad about my life   ____

____-bolsters my confidence when I need it   ____

____-listens to what I have to say   ____

____-tells me what I need to be told   ____

____-seems to know when I need a call   ____

____-never forgets my birthday   ____

____-doesn't make me pay for everything   ____

____-is someone I'd do anything for   ____

____-makes me smile thinking of them   ____

____-likes me for who I am   ____

____-would stand up to for me   ____

____-would stand by me in a dark alley   ____

____-will argue with me…and still be my friend ____

The ranking you completed may alter over the years but the basic foundations that you see in your friendships won't. With each friend that you completed above, how would they rank you if they were completing the same list? Would they feel that you place them on your "B" list? Do they see you as good a friend as you see them? Do you both counter-balance each other's strengths and weaknesses? It's okay to discuss stuff like this with your friends. You might be pleasantly surprised by their responses to exercises like this. If you prioritized properly your A/B/C attributes, then you made a really positive start. **If your friends are not delivering against your A and B priorities then you aren't clearly communicating your expectations or, you have the wrong friends.**

Your posse in life is like a lifeline to the outside world. There will be many people who will go out of their way to cause you grief. They will make it their business to stir up issues around you or to pull you down. I've watched it throughout my life and I've had my fair share of experience on the receiving end. You need your friends to help offset this foolishness, keep you grounded, make you laugh and see the amazing things that life offers. **You need friends who will instinctively show up in a time of need.** Find 1-2 best friends that would give up a kidney for you without stopping to think of the consequences. Do you have friends like this? Is there someone you'd give up a kidney for?

I feel very blessed with the people who I call my friends. They don't make me feel "B" listed and on my list, they are all in the 8-10 ranking level. I'll share one brief story about a friend. Years ago, my wife and I were selling a house and had an agent showing on the same day I was in New York presenting to my head office. The showing was at 1:00 pm. At 10:00 am, that morning, my wife Martha discovered that the basement drainage had backed up and there was an horrific mess about 4 inches deep *everywhere*. Timing for the sale was critical and our agent insisted we proceed with the showing, or the other agents would feel there was a problem with the house. Now, as all husbands reading this will understand, my inside voice was quietly saying, "Thank God, I'm here and don't have to deal with that mess at home!" I could only imagine the disgusting issue that had to be rectified immediately.

I suggested that Martha call our good friend Larry who would know a service that we could get to immediately fix the drain, empty the mess, and get the smell out of our house. All had to be accomplished before 1:00 pm the same day. Martha made the call.

Larry immediately dropped everything he was doing and arrived at our house. He didn't call someone. He came directly to our house and along with Martha, tackled that mess in the basement until the issue was corrected. It was so far "beyond the call of duty" that we hardly knew what to say. After Larry and Martha cleaned, my wife baked chocolate chip cookies and sprayed the house with anything she could find. At 1:00 pm the front door opened and twenty agents arrived. The showing was a success and in short order the house sold. Just for the record, Larry is not a plumber or a construction-type. He owns and runs his own advertising agency except for that specific morning when he became our plumber and helped save an ugly situation. How is that for a friend?

Here's **part three** of the exercise. Go back and complete a second list that includes your family members, business acquaintances and people you hang out with at work. Your prioritization of the attributes should change. You won't have the same expectations of this group. As you complete this exercise, don't ever underplay the relationships that you have with your family members. There is nothing handcuffing you to a family member who abuses their relationship with you. If you have to move a family member in the "C" grouping of people you know...then so be it. It can be permanently damaging for you to maintain relationships with family members who drag you down.

You need to surround yourself with people who help you to be your best...both at home and at your place of work. Galen G. Weston is the Executive Chairman of Loblaw Companies. Recently, he shared the importance to, "look beyond yourself and bring the right people to your team in <u>everything</u> you are doing."

Chapter 21 Key:

No (wo)man is an island. Surround yourself with outstanding people and they will help you achieve greatness. Surround yourself with average talent and you will be mediocre.

Chapter 22

"Love recognizes no barriers. It jumps hurdles, leaps fences, penetrates walls to arrive at its destination full of hope..."

-Maya Angelou

It's really vital that you understand the power of love. A chapter on love in a business book...what's next? I think it's important to talk about love and I won't make light of it, or joke around. If this makes me old-fashioned or sappy, then I'm old-fashioned and sappy. Don't read this chapter if you don't want to.

I believe in love and if you don't, you are missing out on life itself. Don't tell me you've been burned in bad relationships, you hate your father, or you're afraid of divorce. I see it very simply. Finding and protecting love is mandatory for you to be fulfilled in life. **Without love, you are crippling your chances to be fully successful in your career, or truly happy in any relationship you have.**

If you've completed Chapter 1, then you've stepped back and looked at your life: Past, present and future. You've discovered some consistencies and inconsistencies in your beliefs and behaviors. You've thought about all the factors, including family and relationships that are affecting you both positively and negatively. Consider what you just read in the last chapter. Think about your relationships with others for the purpose of understanding that **you are not alone** in this world.

We've all been in screwed up relationships. Some were doomed by our own doing and some beyond our control. We've mixed up lust for love, loneliness for love, and like for love. We've been with people who built us up; people who dragged us down; and frankly, people who just wasted our precious time. I'm sure as some of you are reading this, you are categorizing your significant other into what I just wrote. Whether you have thought about it or not, they are probably categorizing you the same way. Ever thought about that?

Did you learn anything in Chapter 1 that gave you a better understanding of yourself and how you are approaching others? One of my key learnings in life is that **until you know yourself and are almost 100% comfortable with who you are, you can't logically expect to find true happiness with another person.** It just won't happen. Similarly, until you like and love yourself no one else will be able to love you. They may think they do, but it won't last. It all comes down to you understanding the whole "ego" game before you can connect with someone else.

Play an exercise with me...just for fun.

(A) Write down the names of the five people in your lifetime (present and past) that you have loved the most. If possible, prioritize the names. Ignore the brackets on the right for a moment.

1. _____(_____)
2. _____(_____)
3. _____(_____)
4. _____(_____)
5. _____(_____)

(B) Now continue the exercise by writing down the names of the five people in your lifetime (present and past) who you firmly believe(d) loved you dearly.

1. _____(_____)
2. _____(_____)
3. _____(_____)
4. _____(_____)
5. _____(_____)

Compare list (A) with list (B). What conclusions can you draw? Are there different names on each list? Are the priorities different as well? Out of curiosity, did you include family members on your list? It's very interesting if you did not.

For added interest, go back to list (A) and in the bracketed section on the right, note whether each person loved you equally, less or more than you loved them. Complete the exercise for list (B) with whether you loved each of these names equally, less or more than they loved you.

What have you discovered about your lists? About twenty years ago I found myself stuck in a hotel room because of a flight cancellation. Out of complete boredom, I made a list of all the people I had dated in life. It was an incredible exercise. Some brought back wonderful memories. Some didn't. When I added the bracketed section to the list it gave me pause for thought. Very seldom have I felt about someone equally to the way they felt about me. When I looked even deeper at the list, I recognized that there were people on it who should never have made my list. Some personalities were like thrusting kryptonite in Superman's face. Perhaps at that time in my life, they were "time fillers." Perhaps I didn't have the confidence to move on from them when I should have. I can see two names that did nothing but damage my self-esteem and seriously drag down my career. What was I thinking? Perhaps the better question is what part of my body was I thinking with? Conversely, I also see a name or two that I should have respected more than I did.

Anyway, 25 years ago when I finished this list, I found it really disturbing. I had just completed the exercise in Chapter 1 of this book, and as I stared out the window in that hotel room, I began crafting a new game-plan. I could not continue having the kind of relationships that were inconsistent with who I thought I was, and who I wanted to be in the future. With a great deal of soul searching and deliberation, my course of action became crystal clear to me. I discussed my plan with my close friends and to a person, they all agreed.

This exercise had shown me that **it was mandatory that I discontinue the toxic relationship I was in; spend more time with my closest friends; quit my job; find a new job more consistent with my goals; and, meet a woman whose values, goals and dreams were more consistent with my own.** This was a big order to fill but if I didn't tackle every issue, I was going to continue to float in mediocrity. I went at my plan very methodically. Some actions were going to harder than others.

The job action was one of the harder ones to go at. It was a little more frightening because I was in a company and position that felt comfortable, secure and wasn't stretching me too far beyond my limits. The pay was good and steady. I wasn't being overly taxed and I liked my bosses. There was no big upside, and conversely, no apparent big down-side. Sound familiar? All those warm and cuddly things were exactly what I had to get away from. I needed a job that would offer me a really big challenge and upside which meant accepting the corresponding offset. No risk of failure, no chance to make big money, or to push yourself to new limits. I needed a company that would afford me the chance to earn more than just a highly-taxed salary. I needed an equity position. If I was going to have an enduring career, I needed a job that could position me for an international posting. I needed rich, formal training, and a possible pathway to the corner office.

I won't kid you that any of this action-plan was easy because it wasn't. On some days I felt like I was in a de-tox clinic. The first 6 months into my game-plan was like a rollercoaster. I spent a lot of "alone time" re-thinking and honing my plans. I determined that my persistence was going to play a vital role, just as it had in getting my first job at General Foods (Chapter 6). I didn't move off my plan and I diligently sought the kind of work position I needed. At the same time, I quit that lousy relationship and didn't look back once. I kicked up my exercise regiment and cleaned up my act on diet and alcohol. Everything seemed to fall into a very positive place as my plan unfolded. I began feeling more stable, greater harmony and a healthier inner peace. All the pieces of my game-plan were coming together, except for one. I was lonely and knew I had to find my soul-mate.

I met a lot of women, but none of them fit the bill. Eventually, my sister and her former university room-mate came up with a blind date for me. All of you out there know the odds of success when your sibling has set you up on a blind date. That encounter has about as much chance as George Bush being re-elected for a third team. I had supplied a list of twenty attributes I wanted any blind date to possess. Undaunted, the two came across a woman who co-incidentally had a list of her own. They gave me her phone number. I have to be honest that the call didn't go very well. Within minutes we were arguing about something, or other. However, despite the rough start, we agreed to one date and made arrangements. Even that didn't come off without a hitch and because of a snafu in her schedule, she stood me up. I was furious with her, my sister, my sister's friend, and the world.

It was not a promising start for any relationship but something sparked me to try again. Perhaps it was the flowers of apology that she physically taped to my front door. We set another date and I'm glad we did because it led to the best relationship of my life. I was thunderstruck head over heels, and as our friendship blossomed to love, my entire personality shifted. Unforeseen opportunities seemed to fly in my direction: One door after another opened up to me...including a fantastic job opportunity.

It took one really hard and intense year to get my life in order. But once it was in order, my confidence was restored and never left me again. I had learned the benefit of taking control of your own life and not allowing yourself to wallow in a bad job, or in an unhealthy personal relationship. I discovered that there was a soul-mate out there for me and that love did exist if you invest yourself to find it.

I will state with conviction that I would not be a CEO today if not for the love of my wife and children...and the deep love I feel for them. This foundation makes me stronger to face and overcome the obstacles that life and career pound at me daily. My resolve to be my best is untouchable. My sense of adventure grows each year with their support and belief. By the way, I married that girl stuck flowers on my door. We've been happily married for almost twenty years.

Don't miss out in the fullness of the heights your success can reach by trying to go it alone, or by staying in a relationship you know is wrong for you. Figure all this out before you have kids. Don't risk messing up their lives because you haven't got your act in gear. Please don't exist in the short-lived rhapsody of one-nighters, fooling around with married people, or enduring useless relationships that are just filling up your calendars. Look back at Chapter 1 and determine who you want to be. Find the person who can help you achieve that. (S)he may be out there looking for the same thing.

Chapter 22 Key:

I adore my wife and children and without their love I would be nothing. Find true love in your life no matter what you have to do, or wherever you have to go. It's there waiting for you.

Chapter 23

"My wife met me at the door the other night in a sexy negligee. Unfortunately, she was just coming home…"

-Rodney Dangerfield

Here are some considerations and questions for husbands and/or fathers reading this book. You might find something you can use.

1. My best advice for soon-to-be fathers is to learn the following phrase and practice it endlessly until it comes out with well-rehearsed sincerity:

"Yes dear, you're right. I'm wrong."

The timing of the delivery of each word is crucial. If you deliver it properly with the correct amount of well-rehearsed sincerity, it will get you a free get-out-of-jail card until the baby is at least 12 months old. Blow the timing/delivery of the wording and you will be on diaper-duty for life.

2. Your mother-in-law can be your best ally in life or the equivalent of a *"60 Minutes"* crew showing up at the door of your office with their cameras on and America watching. While your mate may slag their mother…you must never do the same thing. You should know that **your wife will become your mother-in-law in due course.** I hope you like your mother-in-law. I adore mine.

3. Having children does not mean you and your wife don't need to have time together anymore. Don't allow the essence of your relationship to ebb. Your children will be very attuned to the strength of your relationship

with your wife. **A successful family needs the firm foundation of a healthy partnership and friendship of the parents.**

4. Regardless of who works and who stays at home, get off your duff and help out around the house. Not just when your mother-in-law or friends are visiting. **Your mate is not your house-keeper so don't treat her like one.**

5. Early in your marriage, your mate and you need to come to a working agreement with regards to money, budgets, religion, inter-family time allocations, present "expectations" and children-rearing approaches. You need to discuss insurance and wills. The longer you leave these discussions, the harder they become later. **Don't avoid discussing the most critical issues.**

6. Never go to bed angry with each other. Come to some resolution even if it is to give the argument some time. You married your best friend. You need to argue with your wife unless you intended to marry a doormat who simply jumped at your every command. Even if you are certain that you are totally correct, and she is 100% wrong, you must be conciliatory and offer an olive branch before the lights go out. *Added bonus...*within 24 hours of that olive branch offering, you will have great sex with your wife. I've always taken this as my wife's acceptance that she was wrong in the first place!

7. You and your wife need time apart or the relationship will stagnate. Absence does make the heart grow fonder. Please carefully read the Chapter 26 on "rejuvenating your batteries and alone time." You also need to plan date nights once the kids come along. Your children and their time commitments will vampire your life. **You must protect your time with your mate.**

8. Agree with your wife that you will present a united front to your children. Never disagree with each other in front of your kids. Take the argument away from them. They will clue in at a very early age if they are able to divide and conquer you.

9. **Be consistent in your messaging to your kids.** Over time, this consistency will provide your children with terrific goal posts and boundaries that they will come to appreciate and work within. Never contradict your mate in front of your children. Deal with differences privately and then

go to the children with a united front. In those events where you find yourself disagreeing with your wife...be respectful.

10. **Don't be afraid to show your affection to your children, or to your wife** in front of your children. Tell them you love them every day of their lives. Find time to read them stories at night and then tuck them in. Hold off on tickling until daylight time...never just before bed. Make sure you given them the chance to talk with you and share anything that is causing them unrest.

11. **Be yourself** in front of the kids. Children have an uncanny ability to sniff out fakeness in adults. Let them see by your example how they should be acting when you aren't around. Speak with, and not "at" them. Don't converse in long diatribes. Speak in short, easily comprehensible phrases. Don't lose your child's attention or make them feel stupid because they don't understand you. Ask them to play back to you what they've heard you say. Listen to all of their questions respectfully, and patiently. Don't speak flippantly with your children.

12. As your kids reach the teen years they will spend a lot of time away from home. This is very disquieting for parents with the fear of drugs, booze, AIDs, STDs, and pregnancies. I always tell my kids to stop and think for a moment when they are faced with a decision. Ask them, **"Would you do this if Mom or Dad were standing right beside you?"**

Chapter 23 Key:

For all men out there: Act like a man...but in a nicer, more considerate manner.

Chapter 24

"Women will never be as successful as men because they have no wives to advise them..."

-Dick Van Dyke

Here are a few considerations and questions for wives and/or mothers reading along.

I have decided that this is the most dangerous chapter for me to write. The opportunity for me to find myself castrated by my wife, daughter, sisters, female relatives, and/ or female co-workers, hangs in the balance with how fine a line I can walk. I do have a few comments to make but allow me to set the stage for my own safety.

Giving advice to a woman, when you are a man, is a very tricky enterprise, unless you are in the world of fashion, design or cosmetics. For the rest of us mere mortals, it's usually a wise move to keep your counsel to yourself. Besides, when you look at the *fashionistas* and cosmetic giants, you know that their advice will always be consistent: You are too fat and too old for society and you'd better do something about it. Their products, as Charles Revlon once put it, *"give hope."* Hope for what?

Years ago, my sister was working her way past a divorce. She was doing it professionally and very maturely. Having left the marriage, she now faced the prospect of re-entering the dating world. Being the younger brother, I was aware that a lot of things had changed in the dating world since she was in it...as I teased her, "sometime around the civil war." Now, talking to your wife or pals about "dating" is one thing. Having a face to face discussion with an older sister is another. When faced with this proposition I decided to make it less awkward for us both by writing down my thoughts for her to consider. I didn't keep a copy but here are some of the things I am sure I shared with her, in one of those "fleeting-younger-brother-caring" moments.

1. **What a man says and what he means are not necessarily the same thing.** For example, if a man asks you at the end of a date if he can walk you to the door...he is asking you if he can come inside. Continuing on with the logic flow...*he's asking if you want to have sex.* Make up your mind on how to answer his "real" question while you are still in the car.

2. When a man says he will call you the next day... *he is lying through his teeth.* Saying you are going to call is a rationalization for getting the hell away from this woman as fast as you can. If a man intends to call, he will. For goodness sakes, don't ask him if he is going to call you and don't ask for his e-mail address. His first reaction is that you are going to stalk him like Glenn Close in *Fatal Attraction*.

3. Men will not want to hear about your kids or your jerk of an ex-husband. Even if they politely ask about your children (if you have any), get on to another topic. Prepare and read the sports pages...even if you can't stand sports.

4. Don't let your first date be at sports bars. Too many televisions to distract him.

5. If a man calls you on Friday for a date on Friday night or Saturday...*he is not respecting you.* Tell him you have a previous engagement. Guys don't like to believe there is competition in the air. Create that expectation even if it's not true. The man needs to call by Wednesday and absolutely no later than Thursday noon. If he calls you any night after 11:00 pm and you can hear the sounds of a sports bar in the background...*he is already half in the bag and isn't thinking of you in a very positive way.*

6. Be very certain of the marital status of the man who you agree to see. Don't beat around the bush. **Don't be fooled by the lack of a wedding ring.** Ask the question outright: *"Are you married?"* Investigate your date prior to going out. It may be possible to Google him and see what he's been up to. Get your female friends to ask their husbands about the man. Don't go

into this blindly.

7. Understanding **STDs is not just a teen-age thing.** If you head into the sexual arena, it is up to you to protect yourself. Remember, if it goes physical, you are sharing with this man every person he has ever been with. AIDS is not a game.

8. **Remember who you are and that you are worth being with.** You don't have to pretend to be someone you aren't. I realize the odds are greatly stacked against middle-aged women who find themselves re-entering the dating world. My brother Bill has actually computed the statistics of this, and it is not a pretty picture for women over forty. For women over fifty, the stats are even worse. Here are the facts. Men in their own age bracket are after younger women. Men in younger age brackets are after the same. It may be necessary to be considering dating men in a slightly older age bracket.

9. When you are on a date with a man he should look at no one but you. If you discover he has a wandering eye that follows every skirt in the room then you have uncovered the truth of what he is all about. Dump him as soon as you can.

10. Arrange first dates in places where you are comfortable. At no time, agree to return to his place on the first date unless you have decided to go physical. Your agreement to "see his place" is telling him you have made that call.

Alright, so far?

I'm feeling my courage pick up a little. Let's get into the gist of this chapter and work through some ideas and considerations for wives and/or mothers:

1. **Men are very different than women. Stop talking to them as if they know what you are thinking. For the most part, we have no idea about anything let alone what you are thinking.** Even when we try to understand what you are thinking, it's not easy. I speak from experience on this one.

2. Don't ask questions that would make Al Bundy squirm. Stop asking us *"Does this outfit make me look fat?"* Who in their

159

right mind wants to tread into the dark and answer that one? I'd rather have my dentist get blind drunk and then perform a root canal on me. I speak for all man-kind on this one. **Stop asking us questions when you don't really want to hear the answer.** If you think the outfit makes you look fat, it probably does.

3. Men need to act like men...not your brother or father. We need to be ourselves. That typically will involve leaving things on the floor, putting dishes in the sink and not the dishwasher, and making funny sounds with all parts of our body. Some of this can be rectified with discussion but not if you simple fix what it is that we've done and then complain about it later. Your simple fix is our way of having you do it anyway.

4. A man can be exhausted from work, fatigued from a late flight home, weary from too many drinks and he will <u>still</u> be up for sex if you look at him sideways. Or for that matter, if you look at him at all.

5. Men don't understand that when you want to talk about something it usually means that you expect them to listen and not offer solutions. Men are fixers, not psychologists. You need to clarify that you don't really want to "talk." You need someone to listen empathetically to what is bothering you. Clarify that you aren't looking for solutions yet. That's fair and will allow your partner to know the game. Personally, I can't listen for more than two minutes without seeing a solution. **God help all men who try to offer up a solution when all that is needed is "an ear."** We can do that if you tell us that's what you need.

6. Men love to wear gym clothes over and over until they have a life of their own. Don't worry about it. Keep their exercise stuff away from your clothes and if possible, outside of the house.

7. If you are dating, see my rules to my sister. **When in doubt, anything that a man says to you is an effort to get you horizontal with the least amount of effort, time and cost.** I know it sounds archaic but that's the reality.

8. If you are married, #4 and #7 still apply most of the time, unless the word "play-offs" is involved in any manner. For Heaven's sakes, don't suggest a movie on the night of a play-off game...in any sport known on the planet.

When you get married, establish the working rules up front from Day One. Your husband is not a crown prince so don't allow him to assume that role within the house-hold. I love how one of my favorite actresses, Bette Davis defined how she'd enter a marriage:

"I'd marry again if I found a man who had fifteen million dollars, would sign over half to me, and guarantee he would be dead within a year..."

Guys work well if the ground-rules are established. Without ground-rules you'll quickly discover your husband's aversion to doing anything around your home beyond manly chores like cutting the lawn, shoveling the snow or taking out the garbage. I think this is the primordial instinct weaving its way back to our cavemen ancestors. Discuss how many times a month you expect to have a date night without friends. Discuss how often you want to go out with your own friends. Similarly, how often is he allowed, oops, I mean, should he plan, to go out with his friends. How will house-hold chores be divided? Write out a list of everything that is required at home. Even if as a couple, you are fortunate enough to have a cleaning lady a couple of times a week, there is still a lot to be done. If you cook then he should clean. If you do the bathrooms, then he should do the vacuuming. If you do laundry, then he should do all garbage and yard work. This is a business partnership with fringe benefits. **Do not become the maid in your own house-hold.** Ground-rules are good for eliminating festering and fights.

9. Don't expect your husband to back down from an argument too quickly. I hope you didn't cheat and read the previous chapter dedicated to Husbands and/or Fathers. That would not be fair for the pearls of wisdom I wrote regarding arguments and the potential aftermath of great sex. Just know one thing--**the more authoritative and loud your husband becomes in an argument, the more likely he feels he is losing it.**

10. Your husband needs reminders of dates that are really important. Don't be silly or proud about this. He will remember his own birthday, Christmas (if it's applicable) and New Years. He has a higher chance of remembering your birthday and anniversary in the first two years of marriage. With each subsequent year, the odds of remembering go down by 10%. By the time you've been

married twenty years, it's all over. Just save time. Either get married on his birthday, or put important dates in his calendar and give him a one week's notice. Why spoil it for him by letting him forget? That's just rude. By the way, **when you get married, you magically adopt the responsibility for sending out all cards and presents to everyone in both of your families.** If you happen to miss someone on "his side," they will hold *you* accountable, not him. Funny how this works, isn't it?

11. Your husband will say inappropriate things about your mother. That's life. Let me explain how this works. Whenever you get into an argument with your wife, some weird button clicks in your head that makes you think about your mother-in-law. In an attempt to clarify your point, you bring her up...usually in what appears to most men, to be an opportune point of the discussion. It usually begins with the phrase, "You are just like your mother." I think the weird button is in reverse, because whatever the intended point of the mother-in-law insertion was meant to be, it never quite comes out that way. Just know that deep inside your husband's mind, his comment about your mother was likely meant as a back-handed compliment. (P.S. Don't ever bring up his mommy).

12. **Stop thinking about Botox, liposuction, face-lifts, and all that total cosmetic surgery foolishness.** Enough is enough. When the lights go out and you are in each other's arms it won't matter what you've had done to your face, breasts, thighs, neck or other regions of your body. Enough with the vanity. Light some candles, turn on some music, throw on some perfume, and show him that there's more to life than surgery. Take all that money you are investing in "upgrading" your looks and plan a really fabulous trip to Paris or Rome...perhaps even with your husband.

13. **Men aren't as tough as they look, sound or act. Inside, we are all sensitive little creatures. Don't be fooled by the rough beard, loud voices or bad smells.** We get emotional during sad movies or when our favorite Idol gets voted off.

14. Help us know what to buy for presents for you. If you want to be a real angel and loving wife...simply buy whatever you want along with some wrapping paper and a reminder of the day/date...give it to us. Save arguments, stress and strain. It won't mean we love you less. Au contraire.

15. Regarding the rearing of children, **don't assume that your husband has more answers than you.** Martha and I determined three things early in her pregnancy with our first daughter that helped us tremendously. First, we wanted to provide consistency in our messaging to our children. Consistency between the two of us was vital so that we wouldn't confuse them with counter directions or answers. Consistency in keeping to the same message and not flipping back and forth as the winds shifted. We knew that this would mean keeping our lines of communication open and being willing to hold off on making a decision in front of our child(ren) until we had a chance to talk. Second, we realized that our relationship and love was the core foundation of our family's unit and that we had to work at it to keep it strong and stable. We needed to plan date nights and vacations apart from our children in order to have the foundation of love and respect be untouchable. I fear that **many parents focus excessive time on careers and their children and ignore themselves and each other**. Their lives revolve around their children's schedules and schooling. It's so disturbing to see friends of children heading off to university at odds with what to do with each other in the empty nest. I remember discussing this with my own father. Dad and Mom spent every day of their lives thinking about the four of us. They scrimped and saved and made every sacrifice in order for us to get ahead in life. I don't remember them ever going off on a week-end alone. Any money went into the house and the needs of their children. Remember why you married your mate. Your children are the outcome of your love for each other. They are not a replacement for each other. Third, we agreed that we would treat our children with the respect of being human beings rather than small children. This sounds a tad strange but it has made all the difference in our children's upbringing. We have always talked, and interacted with our children, like short younger adults. This has helped foster wonderful discussions with them and opened their eyes to the world faster than if we had coddled them or treated them like infants until they were five.

16. For those working wives and/or mothers...I salute you with the amazing amount of respect you deserve. I don't know how you do it. I can't begin to offer advice on this aspect beyond suggesting that you get the help you need from your mate or outside sources. Set parameters at work and be very clear with your boss as to what you can and can't do from a time perspective. If you can't drop the kids off at school and get to your office by 8:30 am then so be it. There has to be flexibility in

this. Don't be feeling guilty about time conflicts between work and home-life. Get the issues out in the open and work with your boss and with your husband to find a solution that can help you to be your best. As your children get older, they become a greater part of the solution in being able to help out more around the house. Don't go this alone.

17. Continue to evolve beyond being a wife and/or a mother. Find the time to constantly be upgrading your skill sets. If and when you find yourself on maternity leave, or fulfilling the role of mother at home, keep yourself at your best. Don't allow your physical or mental fitness to suffer. Strive to keep yourself a hire-able commodity. Maintain your business contacts on a regular basis. Keep a toe in the water for job opportunities. **At all times in your life, your personal well-being depends on you**. Don't ever allow yourself to be caught in a vulnerable situation financially.

18. Take on the finances in your relationship with your husband. Be the contact person with the bank and be able to take out a loan in your name at any time. **Do not give up your banking ability when you get married**. When you buy a house, ensure it either goes in both names, or in your own name. Ensure your husband is adequately insured from day one. Never sign a document without reading it, even if your husband has gone through it and assures you it is okay. You are not a rubber stamp. If you sign your name to a legal document, you are the one accountable, not him.

19. Don't allow festering in your marriage. If you have something on your mind, raise it. Write down what's bothering you and where you can, keep track of specific examples. Hard to argue with facts in writing.

Do men have it easier than women in today's world? I have to answer with a resounding "yes." Will they always?

Chapter 24 Key:

To all women out there: You are the far superior gender. Just don't tell any of my male friends that I've admitted it.

Chapter 25

"I find the harder I work the more luck I seem to have..."

-Thomas Jefferson

Wasting time is wasting your life. Severely managing and controlling time wasters and time optimizers are two of the most critical factors to your success, well-being and happiness. Please pay attention to this chapter and if you follow my suggestions, you will witness a dramatic surge in your energy levels, and life.

1. **Seek out and destroy the activities that are wasting your time.** To do this, you need to analyze over a period of a month exactly how you are spending your time. Set up a daily chart broken out in 30 minute segments. Photocopy this 30 times and fill it out (privately) every noon and before bed. The time analysis includes the moment you wake up to the time you close your eyes in bed. Don't lie to yourself about the chart. This is vital. At the end of the month yellow-highlight the time spent towards your job. Pink-highlight the time spent on your physical wellness (yes, you should include sex under pink). Keep breaking out the activities into chunks represented by various highlighters. Now take a look at your life. Is this how you want to be spending your time? How much of the yellowed job time would you judge was both profitable and successful? How much was wasted and could have been used in a more efficient manner? Are you spending your non-work time exactly how you like to spend it? How much of the non-work time is spent on learning anything new that will help move you forward in life? I don't care what level of seniority you have, or how young/old you are...this is an exercise of common sense that most people don't even consider doing. All we have on this planet is a finite amount of time. Shouldn't you understand how you are expending it?

2. **Write out the name of every person with whom you are interacting at work and socially.** Chapter 21 on "Safety in Numbers," took you through this exercise. Briefly, here's what it said. Rank these people according to what you view as being important in life. Respect, integrity, intelligence, humor...are they *helper-type* people who challenge you to think differently? Could you call them in the middle of the night with an emergency and know that without fail they would be at your door as soon as was humanly possible? Are they the *negative-bent* who are always finding fault? The *cynics* and the *skeptics* whose dark viewpoint of everything is a real drag? Are they the company *politickers* who spend most of their job time plotting out who's in and who's out? Are you seeing your *family members* regularly? Your *Mom and Dad* deserve more than the customary monthly phone call and e-mails don't count where family is concerned. Be brutal on your ranking. Make your "A" list and those are the people with whom you should spend the majority of your time.

3. **Never spin at work.** You must have a written job description and a monthly set of priorities approved in writing by your supervisor. Don't start any task without knowing:

   > exactly what is expected of you;

   >when it is due and what flexibility in the timing exists;

   >how/what delivery format is expected;

   >how the results will be analyzed and used;

   >what the action standards are for your task;

   >what backups are in place in the event your output is not accepted by your supervisor;

   >what budgets you are dealing with;

   >who can help you; and most importantly,

   >the true reason you are being asked to complete the task.

   Again, your level of seniority is irrelevant. If you commence a task not knowing the above questions you are a fool and will not achieve full success. **Don't be afraid to ask questions at the onset of any project or task you accept.** Ensure you are asking the right person the right questions, even if you have to go back a second time for clarification. Cut out any potential for ambiguity. Don't spin and don't let any people with whom you work spin.

4. **Upgrade your skill sets** with actions designed to save you time: Time management courses, speed typing, speed reading. The investment in cultivating your skills will pay back ten-fold. Upgrading yourself is like getting a transfusion of potential pumped directly into your career.

5. **Surround yourself with people who can help you expedite your job responsibilities more efficiently.** Find people who are more efficient and time-aware than you are. Watch from them and learn.

6. **Take an assertiveness training course immediately.** Learn to say no and not feel one ounce of guilt. Learn how not to take on additional tasks without something being removed from your plate. Learn how to delegate upward every time you can. Don't let the people you supervise clean their plate by delegating upward to you.

7. **Plan out your year in advance** and include timing for your vacations, your exercise schedule, your family time, your training/learning time, your heavy work period time, your boss's holiday schedule time, and statutory holidays. Share this with your supervisor and your reports. Have them complete the same exercise. This particular year, once gone, will never come back to you again. The upcoming 365 days are irreplaceable days in your life. Share your plan and protect that time. As you get older, these 365 days start to feel like 355 days...then 345 days. Each of my years seem like they are 250 days...at the most. I don't know how the time flies by so quickly. Planning out your time gives you goal-posts to shoot at. Review your plan every month. Are you on track? If not, what is diverting you that must be addressed? If the answer is, "my job", then you have to step back and tackle the issues head on.

8. **Have people working for you are smarter than you think you are.** I'm amazed at how many people ignore this. People hire ever so slightly beneath their own skill set and intelligence. Lack of confidence? Perhaps. That's how organizations down-grade their overall success. Each level reduces itself in quality. *Hire "above" yourself and you will be promoted faster.* Always consider

that your job is to "work yourself out of that job." It is possible to successfully pursue this philosophy if you are prepared to make the hard calls on staffing. Follow Jack Welch's example at General Electric. Rank the total 100% of your employees as a 20/70/10 based on their performance and potential. 20's being the stars you must retain for your company's success. 70's being the bulk of your employees who you are training to upgrade with experience. 10's being the people who need to leave, or be removed from the company because of poor performance and no upside potential. At evaluation time **it's vital to be candid and honest with each employee at all seniorities.** Let them know where they stand and how the company is ranking them and their future potential. Don't coddle the weaker performers who you are ranking as 10s. They have a right to know where they stand and what they can expect. If you do this properly, they you will be able to focus more time on the stronger performers in the 20s and 70s camps. This extra attention will help them be even better contributors to the company.

Most bosses err and spend the majority of their time and training investment on the 10s which is totally illogical. Eventually, you are going to end up terminating the 10s with heavy severance costs to your P+L. With complete candor to all employees, you will find that about 30% of your 10s will leave on their own and with their reputation protected. You'll also discover that your severance costs will be reduced.

A very wise CEO at BBDO, Tom Clark told me, "*A business is like a battleship, not a cruise liner. Battleships don't carry passengers.*"

9. **Delegation is sharing responsibility--not giving up accountability.** You must learn how to get projects done through other people without giving up ownership. You can't do everything yourself. Frankly, you don't want to do everything yourself. Your team has to grow under, and around you. That won't happen if you have to be the pitcher on the mound at every turn of the game. Does the baseball pitcher pitch the ball and then run behind home plate to catch it himself? Obviously not. Determine where you must be and be there. Determine where you don't have to be, and delegate that. Ensure your expectations are very clearly laid out with action standards and timing for the deliverables. Make yourself available to your team and don't assume everything is going to go well. You must inspect progress on a regular basis

with your own eyes. *You can give up the responsibility but never the accountability.*

10. **Quickie no brainers that have helped me:**

-Don't touch paper more than once. Read and then:

a) file it; b) send it on; or, c) recycle it.

-Respond to every e-mail on the spot...don't leave it for later... you will have to re-read it and remember what you were thinking

-Get into the daily habit of reading only the headlines in a newspaper

-Don't send e-mails longer than 3 short sentences

-Never do the same job twice. Do it correctly the first time

-Don't leave phone messages longer than 20 seconds in length. State your name, number and time and exactly what you need. Don't leave mysterious messages like, "Oh, there's a real problem and I need you to call me."

-Don't have your cell phones on during a meeting...focus on what you are doing

-Encourage your fellow workers or friends to keep any e-mails to you short

-Learn to return calls when you can get the person you are calling to answer the phone. Try early in the morning, lunch time or after dinner

-Be consistent on your timing of arriving/leaving the office

-Never allow friends to keep you waiting more than twice. After giving them a clear warning, dump them for disrespecting you

-Don't ever be late for an appointment. That's downright rude

-Don't have meetings that last longer than one hour

-Go to other people's offices/cubicles for meetings...that way you can get up and leave

-Plan out your evenings and week-end nights weeks in advance

-Get your name off copy lists where-ever possible. If it's important, you'll be found

-Stop reading drivel. Read on an exercise bike. Watch the TV news on a treadmill

-Completely avoid procrastinators at all costs

-Carry around work or something to read in case you get caught waiting with down time

-Don't reinvent things that are already available for you to use

-Extirpate time wasters from your life

Chapter 25 Key:

You have 1440 minutes in each day. 365 days each year. Approximately 85 years in each life. Don't foolishly squander one minute. There is no "gimme" to life.

Chapter 26

"It's a common experience that a problem difficult at night is resolved in the morning after the committee of sleep has worked on it…"

-John Steinbeck

Sleep and having time alone are God's ways of rejuvenating you for the next battle. Sleep is the best remedy in the world for whatever is ailing you whether it is fatigue, stress, sore eyes, a bad cold or depression. The Dalai Lama said that, *"Sleep is the best meditation…"*

Many fears and bad thoughts are borne from fatigue which distorts reality and judgment. I'm amazed that no matter how insurmountable a problem seems one day, it always seems more manageable the next day, after I've managed to get a decent sleep.

How to get a decent sleep? Exercise your brains out. Make yourself physically exhausted. Do something that makes you sweat. Get outside and get fresh air. Tackle a job that gets you dirty. Watch your food and liquid intake. Don't eat or drink after 8:00 pm. No snacks just before hitting the sack. Cut all caffeine at noon, including diet sodas. Go for a walk after dinner. Don't watch programming that might emotionally upset you before bed: Prime example of this…never watch the late news. No one needs that kind of depressing stimulation when you are trying to slow yourself down.

Write down everything that is bothering you on a pad before hitting the sack. Leave it beside the bed along with a pen and nightlight. If you stir…write down what you are thinking, and then roll over. Eventually this exercise will help you avoid festering about issues because your mind will accept that they are recorded. Be consistent in your patterns. Plan the same time to go to bed every night and try to protect that schedule religiously. Get your mind and body trained when it's time to shut down. If you are having trouble sleeping get to a doctor. Do not suffer insomnia. As W.C. Fields quipped, *"The best cure for insomnia is a lot of sleep."*

––––––––––––––––––––

Just as important as getting recuperative sleep every night is scheduling time for you to be alone. I view "alone time" as critical to my personal well-being and sanity. When the world around is closing in, I have to get away...inside my own brain.

It may be hard for your significant other or friends to understand that you need this solitude. They may feel rejected: *"Is it something I've done, or said?"*

Of course it's not something someone has said or done. It's something that is private and healthy for us all. Your S.O. and friends need to be made to understand that this exercise will make you stronger and healthier, so that the time you do spend with them, will be better for you all. You simply want to be your best for yourself and for them.

I preciously protect my "alone time" and my wife and children are very respectful of it. I've learned to incorporate this time into my running schedule, my work-outs, or daily walks with our dog, Ginger. It's time for me to shut out the world and give my brain a chance to slow down from Warp Drive. I can ignore company issues be they financial, client or staff-related. I close the doors on the negativity, and just as anti-oxidants cleanse germs from my body, the sights and smells of the world around cleanse my mind. I love Steven Wright's sense of humor. He talks about alone time when he says, *"I was trying to daydream but my mind kept wandering."*

When my mind is in its "wandering state," I focus on my breathing and what I'm looking at. I go to my "nice" tapes of memories that warm me. I think of happy occasions with my family and friends. I remember favorite movies and songs. Many people practice this as Yoga, Tai Chi or dance. Some say that golf is a perfect escape for them. Not for me though. After I leave the golf course, I have to have some down time to unwind and re-think my lousiest golf shots. Perhaps it will be different in my retirement!

Try to schedule "alone time" once every day. You can do it. You might have to get up a little earlier. You might have to re-arrange some lunches so you can get outside and go for a walk.

Let me share with you a story about "alone time" and my Grandmother. Her name was Margaret Lister and she was ancient when I was born. I used to tease her by calling her Maggie. When I was a little guy, pre double-digits, my Grandmother was well into her eighties. Her age didn't prevent her from coming out to play baseball with me. Boy, could she hit a ball and then cackle like an old hen as it flew over my head. My friends were all amazed at my Grandmother's baseball hitting and throwing.

One evening after dinner, Grandma Lister promised to play some catch, after she finished with her rosary. For those of you who don't know, a rosary looks like a necklace made of beads with a crucifix at the end. Each bead represents a prayer. My Grandmother was raised a very strict Roman Catholic and completed her rosary every night. On this particular evening, I sat beside her with the hope that my presence might make the prayers speed through at a faster pace. I was dying to play ball and my 8:30 pm bed time was soon approaching. Despite my intentionally loud "exhaling," Grandma continued to methodically move onto the next bead. She normally did twenty of them except on Sunday and Holy Days when she would complete the entire rosary...sometimes twice.

Finally, after an eternity of prayers and my bed-time now only twenty minutes away, Maggie looked down at me through her bottle-thick glasses and smiled that amazingly genuine smile that Grandmothers hold in reserve for their youngest Grandson.

"Twenty beads again tonight?" I asked respectfully, trying desperately not to betray my impatience.

"Yes Howie, twenty beads tonight," she replied, as she gathered up the rosary and put it back into the black change purse that had belonged to my grandfather when he was alive.

We sat for a moment and I realized that she didn't seem to be getting up to play ball. I asked a question.

"Is each bead for a different prayer?"

She smiled and nodded slowly as she took her glasses off and cleaned them on her apron.

"Yes they are. The first is for your Grandpa who is in Heaven. The next four are for your Mother and her sisters. The next five beads and prayers are for their husbands and our Priest that they all be good men. Five more are for all of my Grandchildren, including you. The final five are for all the people in the world who don't have enough to eat."

It should have been a very touching moment for me, but with all the understanding of a 9 year-old, I looked up at her, tilted my head and asked,

"And that took up a whole hour?" I demanded, in my most exasperated voice.

Grandma Lister laughed so hard I thought her dentures would fly across the room. She looked me up and down and finally reached over and took my hand in her own.

"No young man, it didn't take *a whole hour.* It only took about thirty minutes."

"Thirty minutes! But you've been sitting here for an entire hour. What have you been doing for the last thirty minutes?" I cried out impatiently, feeling robbed of my baseball time with her.

"Oh, I went somewhere else." Puzzled, and completely thrown off, I looked around and asked, "Somewhere else?"

"Yes son, somewhere else...in my mind."

"Where?" I asked, looking around.

Grandma Lister sighed and stretched her arms above her head. She leaned down and quietly whispered to me:

"That's for me to know and you to find out."

My Grandma Lister lived a healthy life until she was in her early-90s. I've often thought of her life over those 9 decades. Her world changed from horse-drawn carriages and a farm to a world with electricity, automobiles, the Great Depression, two World Wars, Korea, Vietnam, telephones, televisions, Elvis, elevators, Valentino, airplanes, rocket ships, the Beatles, dishwashers, and men landing on the moon. Nuclear bombs were invented and exploded. A Cold War came and went along with society's respect for the elderly. What an incredible amount of stimulation for any one human to have to absorb in her life time.

As a kid, I always figured that given all this incredible evolution, wherever Maggie went for those 30 minutes after her rosary time must have been a pretty happy place to be. Now with more five decades under my belt and my own need for "alone time", I know that to be the case.

Chapter 26 Key:

Take great care to rejuvenate your body, mind and soul every day. You must allow yourself to recharge through a good sleep and "alone time." Find those places my Grandmother escaped to and you'll be a happier and healthier person.

Chapter 27

"He who is frugal is the richest of men, and the miser the poorest..."

-Chamfort

Don't spend what you haven't got. Don't ever spend money to try to impress another person. If that's what it takes to impress them, then they aren't the kind of people with whom you should be spending time. I've noticed that people spend more attention and greater care to their company's financials then they do their own. What foolishness. If you can't afford to buy the car because of the insurance costs, ludicrous gas prices, or upkeep, then don't buy a car. If you can't afford to be shopping at Harry Rosen, Brooks Brothers or Holt Renfrew, then shop somewhere else. There's more than one way to skin a cat and protect your money. In Canada, you're going to be taxed to death at over 50%+ (when you add in every tax on every item you buy). Whether you are 45 or 25 you need to tighten up your belt and pay attention to every dollar passing your hands so you can be targeting to invest in your financial future.

Without having met you, I guarantee you are wasting at least 15% of your disposable income on an annual basis: Probably much more. No need to argue with me on this one. **It's a fact that you are wasting money**. As you progress through life and career and your earnings increase, so will this wastage. Your expenditures and wastage increase with your salary. Sounds pretty mundane, doesn't it? You can argue that with your life and career evolving, you now have children, a house and all the wonderful outlays that go along with that success. I agree. The fact remains that you are still wasting money you don't need to be wasting. Here are considerations that might help stop some of the bleeding and help your future be a more financially solvent:

1. **Prepare a budget.** If you are married, then prepare it with your mate. This will not be a pleasant experience, but if you do it correctly, the two of you will have some major eye-opening discoveries. Your budget should not have "miscellaneous" categories. Account for all expenditures without passing judgment on each other. The budget should be set up monthly and should be reviewed and actualized quarterly. In their book, *"The Millionaire Next Door,"* authors Thomas Stanley and William Danko write, *"How can well-educated, high-income people be so naïve about money? Because being a well-educated, high-income earner does not automatically transfer into financial independence. It takes planning and sacrificing."*

2. **Determine your financial goals.** How much money do you want to save now, and in the future? What will you do with that money? How much money should be invested and at what various risk levels? Set realistic goals but don't make them too conservative or aggressive.

3. **Don't overextend yourself or place a guarantee on your income.** This most recent recession (that no one seems to admit we're in) is a prime example of costs rising and jobs being vulnerable. Being overextended and solely reliant on one job without a "trap door" is folly. Don't spend or invest money that it is causing you to lose sleep, or be in constant strain with your mate.

4. **Target to save no less than 30% of your after tax paycheck.** Set up an automatic withdrawal system to avoid the temptation of spending the money. If possible have the savings removed at source.

5. **Ensure your company is with-holding the proper amount of tax from each paycheck.** No need for surprises at tax time...good or bad.

6. **Don't loan money to anyone under any circumstances.** Especially to family members. *Money and blood do not mix.*

7. **Stop eating at so many restaurants.** Stop buying your coffee at places that charge more than a $1.25 a cup. Make your own coffee at home. Are you so insecure that your image depends on being seen holding a branded coffee cup? Eat breakfast before you leave your home. It's a lot healthier and cheaper than the alternative. It seems some people are agreeing with this given

the number of Starbucks that are closing down.

8. **Budget to donate no less than 5%** of your after tax earnings every year. Please read Chapter 31 on giving back.

9. **Never buy anything full price.** I drive my father insane with my attitude about bargaining, but you'll never save money if you don't try to talk the seller into lowering their price. Watch for sales and never buy something because "you have to have it." Be prepared to walk away from every purchase. Politely ask for "manager discounts" when you buy. Investigate outlet malls. I've found great deals by driving a little out of the way. Saving a buck is a really fun and motivating experience. It's like hunting but without killing something.

Decide how and on what items you are prepared to "spend up on." Similarly, decide on items that you can actually "go cheap on." It's all a matter of deciding what's really worth your dollar. Why are the Wal-Marts and Targets of the world growing so dramatically? Ever check out the kind of cars people drive to Wal-Mart? Take a look. Bunches of Mercedes, Lexus and BMWs lined up in both parking lots. People are opting to save money on items in which they just don't put a lot of merit. These same people will spend their brains out on items that they view hold a special value to them (i.e. their car). **What are the items that you value and the items that don't hold merit for you?**

Do you fully understand the emotional and psychological binds of "conspicuous consumption?" I learned the term *conspicuous consumption* in a Grade 12 Economics class. Very simply stated it means buying stuff for the sake of showing others what you bought. It's displayed vanity with a price tag.

Growing up, my family didn't have a lot of money and didn't really have the first clue about buying a product because of the brand name. The world of branding through advertising was just beginning to explode in the late 50s and 60's through television. Even so, when you didn't have a lot of dough, you bought what you needed at the least expensive price. My parents were very thrifty shoppers having lived through the Great Depression. Their own upbringings taught them the value of a dollar. Even as a kid, I understood that same value until my vanity rose up in Grade 9 and at the tender age of thirteen, I became a victim of "conspicuous consumption." I had a real hard lesson on why never to buy things for show. Let me tell you about it.

I was an average athlete in High School. I had accelerated during Grade School and entering Grade 9 was at least one year younger than my school mates. In some cases, I was two years their junior. On top of this age disadvantage, I was unusually short, thin and admittedly immature for the group. I watched the other guys excel at sports while I couldn't make a team. I watched my more athletic class-mates wearing *Adidas* run circles around the rest of us...especially around me. It was humiliating for a kid in the horrible midst of puberty to be the runt. If only I had those *Adidas,* then I'd show them. The shoes were almost $35.00 which was money I didn't have. It was a small fortune. My folks tried to dissuade the purchase and I just wouldn't understand why Mom and Dad couldn't see the importance of this acquisition. I became so focused on those shoes that I could think of nothing else. I became consumed with envy for every kid I saw wearing them. Finally after relentless badgering, my parents succumbed and we purchased the sneakers. I thought I had died and gone to Heaven. I'm sure I wore them to bed that very night.

The next day, looking forward to showing off, I showed up at school with my new blue sneakers with the trademarked 3 bright white stripes. I couldn't wait to get to school. I came marching down the hallway like a peacock in full feather. I expected admiration and respect. I knew everyone would now look at me differently. Well, they sure did look at me differently... but not how I had imagined. When I walked down that hallway, *it was a disaster*. The reaction was immediate and overwhelming. I was mocked rambunctiously by everyone...especially the more athletic of the students. The onslaught was vicious.

"Breen's got Adidas! Why the hell would you have those? Only real athletes have Adidas. You're useless at sports."

The abuse and bullying continued into the afternoon.

"Breen, you're still crap on the basketball court. Why don't you give those sneakers to someone who can use them?"

That day went on forever and the sting from it still lingers painfully in my mind. I got dirty looks in the school hallway from students who I didn't even know. I finally was so browbeaten and humiliated that I took off the Adidas and shoved them in my locker. I didn't even wear them home, nor did I share with my parents what had transpired that day. I skulked off to my room under the pretense of doing homework. I came out for dinner and then buried myself away for the rest of the night. How could I tell my parents that I never intended to wear those Adidas ever again in life?

But it gets better. To add insult to injury, the shoes were stolen from my school locker. My heart broke when I opened the locker door the next morning and discovered the theft. I reported it to the Principal and phoned home. For three days I was the laughing stock of the school. I found magazine ads of Adidas taped to my locker and shoved in my school books.

More importantly, something else came to light during a discussion with my older sisters. I was asked, "Did you ever stop to think of how the purchase of your Adidas affected our house?" Being self-centered to a fault, my obvious reply was "No." My sisters informed me that the $35.00 spent on the sneakers was about half of the money that Mom and Dad had to spend on the entire family for that week. It was a kick in the guts. I had never stopped to think of that. It was just money and I <u>needed</u> to have those Adidas. My sisters also went on to explain that the $35.00 was probably more than Mom and Dad had spent on themselves in the past six months.

It was one of those defining moments in my life. **I had spent money we didn't have on something that in the end, made me look like a pretentious fool**. After four days, the damned shoes were found in the possession of an older kid. He got kicked out of school for breaking into my locker. As the story unfolded, he hadn't stolen the shoes to wear them. He intended to sell them for the money because his family was in need. I was stunned to hear this...and ashamed. This kid gets kicked out of school and marked as a thief because of my ego.

I would ask you to think about your purchasing philosophy. Do you buy products just for the sake of buying them? Does your wallet or credit card come whipping out without hesitation? Do you compare-shop? Do you look for bargains and sales? Are you prepared to walk away from a purchase if it doesn't make sense? I know I drive my wife insane when we discuss purchasing anything. I can't forget from whence I've come and in particular the lessons of my *Adidas*.

More people are wising up to how they are allocating their funds. With the economy fighting stagflation as it is, people are focusing their purchasing on what they are considering vital. Other purchases are falling into the category of "get it as cheaply as humanly possible or don't buy it." Consciously, or sub-consciously, people are prioritizing every item they purchase and deciding what doesn't deserve to be bought at a higher price. Please consider this:

1. I am not trying to sound "holier than thou." I'm encouraging you not **to fall into the conspicuous consumption trap** just because you can. I'm also suggesting your understand how this affects people around you including your customers and family member. Curb your voracious appetite for expensive purchases.

2. **Never invest in a hot stock pick** or a "sure winner" at the track. By the time any of us normal people hear about a hot tip it's too late. Be very careful whose advice you are listening to when it involves your money. My attitude on investing on "sure things" is to only put in an amount of money I am equally prepared to see go down the drain. Then when I lose it, I feel less stupid. I love Warren Buffet's two key rules:

   Rule No. 1: *Never lose money*.

   Rule #2: *Never forget rule No. 1.*

3. **Understand all the various revenue sources** that might augment your income and for Heaven's Sake, understand the pros and cons of debt from mortgages, bank loans to credit cards. In the States, Americans have a lovely tax advantage of being able to write off a portion of the interest they pay towards their mortgage. That's not a benefit shared by Canadians. Understand the danger to your budget that paying interest on anything will create.

Chapter 27 Key:

Money is hard to come by. Don't waste it foolishly on your ego or bad advice. Treat it as you would your oxygen tank in outer space. In this time of stagflation, determine what you want to spend up on, what you can spend down on...and what you can avoid buying altogether.

Chapter 28

"He who knows when he can fight and when he cannot, will be victorious..."

-Sun Tzu

"If you stand on the banks of the river long enough, the dead bodies of your enemies will float by." This wonderful Chinese proverb is one that I repeat to myself on a regular basis. The fact is that you will have people in life you don't like, and for some reason, won't like you. Curiously, sometimes there will be people you like but who won't like you. That's reality. This chapter is going to talk about that group of people who either: a) don't like you; and/or, b) act in an unacceptably aggressive manner towards you. We've all had them, or have them, in our lives: Bullies. It's important we talk about bullying and how it can affect you and your loved ones. **A bully is like a disease that can severely hamper your career, your happiness and your life.**

"Bullying is a form of aggression involving the abuse of power in relationships. On a global level, it has many faces, including the use of emerging technologies and varies by age, gender and culture. Bullying starts early and its impact lasts a lifetime." (Peplar and Craig 2000).

From the time you are born, you face bullying by siblings. When you spend your first time away from your mother at playgroups or Kindergarten, you will be exposed to bullying. At school, you will see physical bullying as the kids jockey for position like wolves in a pack. Through grade school, high school and even in university you will witness physical bullying. In any school, you will encounter teachers who are bullies...and possibly, teachers who are bullied by parents or other teachers. With your job, there will be co-workers who go out of their way to ensure you know their role and superior position to your own. Every one of you has had, or will have, a boss who uses unfair tactics to pressure you to conduct yourself "his/her way." Possibly to work overtime when it's not really called for…to work the week-end just because (s)he can make you do it. We've all had our share of bosses like that.

Complete strangers can be bullies. It's not uncommon to see reports in the news of road rage incidents where innocent drivers are hurt, and sometimes even killed by another driver over a conflict on the road. Bullies don't just exist to torment you when you are young in school. They don't just appear in lower income housing areas. They don't all have greasy hair and bad teeth. They can be highly educated, socially-aware and highly respected people for whom you work. They can especially be your CEO or other very "strong voices."

In *"Selling the Invisible,"* author Harry Beckworth writes, *"Chances are your organization runs on the Alpha Principal. Ideas do not follow the good thinking in the organization. Ideas follow the power…The Alphas dictate what the group does and thinks…"*

Bullies can be anyone including the church priest, your minister or your rabbi. They can be your neighbors, parents of kids with whom your kids go to school. They can be your significant other. In some cases, they can be your children. They can be a police officer who pulls your over for a ticket. Bullies can be anyone at any time and any place.

A very important conference on bullying was held in Kanderstag in June 2007. Participants representing nations from around the world came together at the "Joint Efforts Against Victimization Conference." I've been fortunate to have read the report and here are the five major points that I took away.

1. It's estimated that over 200 million children around the world are being abused by their peers.

2. It is the moral responsibility of adults to ensure that children's rights to being respected and safe are honored and promoted.

3. The mental and physical health, social and academic consequences of bullying have an enormous impact on human and social capital. The cost of bullying burden our education, health care, social services, and criminal justice systems, as well as work force productivity and innovation.

4. 30% of chronically victimized kids do not tell any adults what is happening to them.

5. Peer intervention only happens around 10% of the time bullying occurs. Note that almost 60% of the time that peers intervene, the bullying stops.

Bullying has now moved into the 20th and 21st Centuries with a vengeance. **With technological advances come new vehicles for people to commandeer to usurp power over others.**

Cyber-bullying is a recently new word that has arisen with great speed since the arrival of MSNing, MySpace and Facebook. The outbreak of cyber-bullying is reaching terrible proportions. I'm sure you can recall the story of Megan Meier, even if you may not remember the name or the details. Megan was the 13 year-old girl living in Missouri who in 2006 was driven to take her own life. She was cyber-bullied to death through the Internet. It all began when Megan met who she believed to be a 16 year-old boy on MySpace. They began exchanging messages and became "pen pals." Megan was happy for the new friendship, especially with an older boy. In reality, her pen pal was neither a 16 year-old, nor a boy. It was a deceitful, twisted adult woman who lived down the street from the Meier family. Cowardly and hidden by her disguise through a keyboard, the older woman first befriended Megan and established a trust and comfort. Then, Iago-like, the older woman turned on her victim viciously. What had been friendly messages turned to intensely aggressive bullying in an open forum that other students were able to observe. Following their predatory instincts and mob-mentality, Megan's fellow students joined in the cyber-bullying like a school of piranha in a feeding frenzy. This woman and the other children might as well have physically dragged Megan to the ground, pummeled her half-senseless on the front steps of the school, and then physically raped her. The vicious taunting was unfathomable and unbearable for a 13 year-old to endure. She felt she had no one to turn to. She was helpless to the relentlessly devastating humiliation. In complete and utter despair, she took her own life. The media jumped all over the story and the reaction from the general public was one of shock and deep concern. Unfortunately, at the time the story broke, the authorities weren't certain how to proceed legally. There were no precedents to follow. Only recently, the authorities have taken action to determine the legal ramifications of this death and any legal action that should be taken on the neighbor. I hope their intentions are firm, just and swift. Unless legal precedents are created, Megan's death will be for naught and this will re-occur.

Recent studies conducted by University of Toronto Professor Faye Mishna show results in line with most other professional research:

-21% of kids say they have been recently bullied on-line

-almost 30% have witnessed bullying of others on-line

Professor Mishna's research feeds back that kids who bully on-line aren't necessarily the kids who would ever bully face to face. Does this not mean that now your kid has to face two different groups of bullies every day at school, and night at home?

So what do you do? Think back carefully. Were you bullied as a kid? I was bullied mercilessly and I remember the embarrassment of every episode. Those memories still scar me today and affect my actions towards others...particularly people I see trying to impose their will on others. Are you being bullied now? Are your children being bullied physically, emotionally or through their computers? Please involve yourself at home with your children. If you are a senior manager in an office, involve yourself in your company to track down where the bullying is occurring. Notice I didn't say "if" bullying is occurring in your office. I'd bet heavy that you have bullies operating around you right now. Let's focus on our children first.

A) Are your children interacting through the internet with other students? Do you have any idea what they are saying or what is being said to them? Find out.

B) Do your children fully understand about sexual predators and how they use the Internet to entrap children? Do you fully understand it?

C) **Bullying through the internet is as painful and damaging as a punch in the gut, or a snub at school.** Neither is acceptable behavior and your children must know that help is available.

D) **Your children must know that they are not alone.** Megan felt she was alone in life. Make sure your children understand this the moment they feel victimized. You should be their first line of defense. The school and school board should be second. Print off any bullying incidents and take this record with you to the school principal. Many Provinces and States have "Safe School Acts" that include bullying in any manner, including cyber-bullying. If there are threats involved it is a matter for your lawyer and the police. **Keeping your head low and hoping this bullying will all go away will not prove to be a successful tactic.**

E) If you are being bullied or (sexually) harassed, don't bury your head in the sand. You are a victim. **No one has a right to dominate you whether it's an employer, a fellow employee, a relative or someone in your neighborhood.** Get to the proper authorities. This victimization will not go away on its own. The damage that this can do to your emotional, physical and mental well-being could be long reaching and ever-lasting. Don't allow yourself to be subjugated by anyone for any reason. Another's repugnant behavior is no excuse for you to be hurt. You are worth more than that.

F) PrevNet is an incredible organization in Canada that acts as a beacon for bullying information and counsel. Go to www. Prevnet. ca for more information. **You are not alone.**

Chapter 28 Key:

Bullies, like cockroaches are a fact of life. They endure. So must you. Do not allow bullies to turn you or your family into victims. Seek professional help and deal with them. Bullies can destroy your career, health and life. Don't put up with them.

Chapter 29

"Power tends to corrupt, and absolute power corrupts absolutely..."

-Lord Acton

How do you survive working for an incompetent idiot of a boss who may or may not know (s)he's an idiot? Most of us have had them. If you haven't yet had an idiot for a boss in your career, you will. Talk about a major obstacle that can cause you to take you eye off your goals! Very early in my career, I had a boss who was an absolute travesty of a human being, and as a manager. Let's make up a name and call him "Bob." Bob oversaw a large division in a company known for its professionalism and marketing expertise. I soon learned by hard experience that he was the black sheep of the company family. He had such a warped sense of life, that he took great pride in embarrassing employees in front of their peers and subordinates. From his corner office, Bob would scream out the name of someone he wanted. You would hear his rants all the way down the corridor. Bob seemed to relish in finding faults with people and then sharing those faults in a public forum, with the sole intent of embarrassing the employee. In his own little mind, Bob's opinion was not to be questioned and he obviously felt that denigrating his staff was fair game. His behavior projected that he was God's gift to intelligence and marketing. I'll admit that Bob was a pretty smart guy for being such a bully and revolting supervisor. Even looking back after thirty years, I remember a lot of his strategic theories and marketing approaches. Although they are somewhat outdated today, they were pretty sharp for that time period. However, while superior leadership skills were not in his cards...deformity of character was.

Every Friday at 5:00 pm, Bob would religiously sit outside the door to his office on his secretary's desk. Everyone who worked for him in his division had to physically pass by him to escape for the week-end. It was like running a "one man gauntlet." Walking down that long corridor to where Bob sat was less preferable than being sentenced to an extended visit with Alfred Dreyfus on Devil's Island.

One of three things would happen. First, you might be corralled for a discussion with Bob on whatever was on his mind. That could hold you in detention for another hour. Second, you might manage to get by him with a nod and a curt word about it being the week-end again. The third option was the worst and most dreaded by us all. This idiot of a boss would nail one to two employees to complete some whim of an assignment. Invariably, the assignment was due back to him first light Monday morning. Whatever your week-end plans had been, were now for naught. No excuses would be accepted and this was your "penance" for being in his division...the colonoscopy your doctor orders you to take.

I was nailed three times for the week-end patrol and I was just too young and inexperienced to tell him to take his week-end assignment and shove it. Either that, or in my extreme junior position my instincts for the survival of my career told me to shut up and just get it done. I realized that this inept bully of a boss was in a position to send my burgeoning career careening down the wrong path. Bob's was the ultimate signature within the division on my evaluation and timeline for promotion. I always wondered why the senior executives in the company put up with this abhorrent behavior. They were aware of his shenanigans and would discuss it in public forums. I could not understand why they didn't hold Bob culpable for his actions. Their lack of attention to rectify this poor management approach was as unprofessional as the manager himself. Their silence condoned behavior which led to a number of really strong performers leaving the company, when their self-esteem could stand it no longer. Although many of us discussed "going over Bob's head" it was a different generation in business where any such insurrection would not have been tolerated.

After too many years of this tomfoolery, he quit or was fired and the bells rang throughout the company. Bob organized his own going away gathering in his office. It was on a Friday at 5:00 pm! Can you believe the irony of that? Given the guilt instilled into me as a kid by the Catholic Church, I showed up at 5:15 pm to find him in his office. Like a kid sitting alone at his own birthday party, Bob jumped up from his chair...genuinely thrilled to see me. I sat with him for 15 minutes hoping some other guilt-ridden co-worker would come along to say good-bye. Within minutes he started berating me about something or other, and I politely made my excuses and left. I saw Bob years later at some industry function and he beetled his way across the reception area and greeted me like an old friend. His demeanor was so friendly that I had to take a step back from him. His career had dried up as his reputation preceded him like the black plague. He looked much older and haggard than the demigod we had all mistaken him for. He was mid-stream in a divorce. I often wonder if God gave him a mulligan in life, would he realize what an idiot he had been in his own fiefdom?

I've had other bosses that fit this category of being idiots like Bob. I could probably write an entire book about them. **Not all bosses are created equal. When you find a terrific boss who is cerebrally-gifted, professional, inspirational, and just, you've got yourself a treasure.** Stick with that person. What do you do when your boss drives you to distraction with his/her unprofessionalism? Here are some things to consider:

1. **Remember your long term goals.** This is a short-term obstacle if you play your cards intelligently. You can quit any time you want to. Remember that. You are in charge, not him/her.

2. **Simply because someone is your boss does not give them any license to treat you with disrespect personally.** They may put you through hell with workload and attitude, but they may not publicly show you any disrespect.

3. **The word "boss" does not mean superior.** It usually means more seniority and experience in the company.

4. **You can learn as many valuable lessons from an idiot boss as you can from a superior boss** if you approach this with a strong mindset. I would rather be learning from the latter group who make life and business more motivating. Who wouldn't? When you find yourself working under an inferior boss, attack the situation as a learning experience. Rationalize that it will fit into your long term goals. Watch their inadequacies and work ethics. Watch how they deliver in their accountabilities and get things done. There will be strengths in how they perform their duties. Learn them and decide what of their approach and ethics you will pick up and which you will never emulate, or tolerate.

5. **Document everything** that occurs between you and your

supervisor and keep discs and files at home. Write down, and date, every unpleasant or rude interaction. Write down every positive and negative comment made about your contribution and performance. Make a note on every slag your boss makes on other employees, peers, or his superiors. This document may prove invaluable to your protection in the organization; with interaction you may have with the HR/Personnel department; or, with your lawyer if you boss moves to terminate you.

6. As you would with any boss, ensure you have a **documented job description and that every week you update and document your progress and deliverables.** Include any project requirement or timing changes and note when the projects were concluded and any learning for future projects.

7. **Don't allow your boss to overload you with projects or to impose timelines that are not achievable.** Taking on more work to avoid an unpleasant interaction with your boss is utter stupidity. You are destined to fail. **How can you do your best work when you allow yourself to spread thinly across too many deliverables?** If a mandatory project comes your way, then politely but firmly demand that something be removed from your list. At the least, the deadline on a current project should be extended to allow you to invest the proper amount of time and energy. My rule of thumb is simple. One project added means one project needs to be removed or delayed.

8. **Set a time limit of how long you are prepared to work for this idiot boss.** Remember, it's your career and no one has a gun to your head to make you stay. Continue to investigate options on the street in case something goes awry. Never quit out of anger. If you have to remove yourself from the situation for a couple of days then call in sick. Use the time at home to get some work done without interruptions and to gather your wits. Sometimes a short break from the office allows you to fortify your resolve.

9. **Build relationships with as many people in your organization as possible.** Without prostituting yourself, try to take on roles away from your daily accountability and the idiot boss. Offer to engage in company training/education. Be seen as an employee willing to invest his/her time in over and above projects designed to move the company ahead. Build a reputation as a positive influence. Never denigrate your boss, or their working style. Keep your counsel to yourself. Others employees or executives will be totally aware of your situation and will be watching how

you conduct yourself. This is definitely a case where discretion is the better part of valor.

10. Once you've escaped from being under the auspices of this idiot, remember your lessons well. **Promise yourself never to conduct yourself in the same manner...don't become an idiot boss yourself.**

Chapter 29 Key:

Idiot bosses are put on this planet to make our lives miserable while we're stuck with them. Get a plan to protect yourself and escape from their dictatorship. Promise never to treat your employees the way they treated you.

Chapter 30

"Think how many blameless lives are brightened by the indiscretions of other people..."

-Saki

There is really nothing indiscreet about a question...the only indiscretion is in your answer. How many times have you found yourself facing someone who relentlessly asks questions you'd rather not answer? Why do most people feel compelled to answer? Why do people give responses that they know they will later regret?

When you find yourself in this "questioning" situation, either socially or professionally, catch your breath, but don't answer the question. There is no gun being held up to the side of your head. No one can force words from your mouth unless you are totally naïve, or devoid of tact. Some people out there have an uncanny ability to ask the most embarrassing and uncomfortable questions. Certain people get paid to do this for a living. Others do it for personal entertainment or kicks. Finally, there are those that do it without fully understanding the discomfort they are creating with their questions. Let's talk a little about each group.

For the former "professional" interviewers, I propose that you be prepared at all times. You must **never be lulled into an "off the record" conversation with a reporter.** When you state something, be prepared to see it on the front page of the New York Times. If you are in a position of representing your company publicly, then I suggest that you immediately schedule PR media training to help you prepare. If you've already had what you believe to be the proper media training, then schedule "top-ups" on a bi-annual basis. It's a really good reminder for you to not fall prey to an innocent question that might lead up to a series of punishing right hooks speeding towards your face. Regular media training will keep you on your toes. The training will also remind you of the critical importance of having positions that you wish to be recorded, regardless of what questions are posed to you.

With a team of seasoned experts, I would also suggest you **prepare yourself and your company for a list of potential press disasters that could come your way.** Discuss how you and your company would manage each situation, and then carefully document the questions and answers. Determine the 5 bullet points that you would be responsible for promoting in the company's public voice. Keep these written Q+As accessible. Place a copy under your phone or key board. Leave one in your office desk at home. Always be prepared.

Control the timing of any interviews you have. Don't allow the reporter to catch you off-guard on the phone. If possible, ask the reporter for a list of questions in advance to allow you to better prepare your answers. Have them e-mailed to you and then gather input from your senior team. If you do receive the questions in advance, prepare other questions knowing the reporter will likely try to catch you off guard. Stick to your prepared answers regardless of what you are asked. Controlling the time of the interview means never getting drawn into an interview when you are ill, tired or hungry.

What about when the interview is underway and you find yourself feeling badgered…hearing the same question repeated *at* you time again. The interview has taken on the air of an interrogation. Do not display attitude or frustration and do not be sucked into becoming a combatant. Maintain an even keel and keep to your script. It's perfectly acceptable to respond with, "I believe that question has been asked and answered. What's your next question?" If the reporter persists then politely, but firmly, re-iterate, "Next?"

Let's move on to the second group of "interviewers." These are the un-paid inquisitors who ask uncomfortable questions for their own self-service. Some people just love to be provocative and see what they can stir up. Putting you on the defensive creates a protective layer for their insecurities. Your response to these people depends on several factors, including where you are and who is within listening distance. Who is this person asking the question? Are they important to your career or family? If the answer is "yes" to these two questions then you must address the person with a diplomatic answer that reveals no more than you feel comfortable with. If they persist, then firmly move to change the topic as many times as it takes until they cease the interrogation. Find a reason to excuse yourself and then return and engage someone else in a conversation. If the interrogation continues then you must address it in a frontal and crystal clear fashion.

"I know you aren't intending it, but this conversation is making me feel uncomfortable so let's move onto another topic, okay?"

Just like that. A well-placed smile will deliver the message and show you aren't angry. You just aren't going to be baited or toyed with.

If the person is not someone critical to your career or family then the response is different and much more direct. There is still no reason for rudeness or unprofessionalism. I simply smile, say I'm going to freshen my drink and excuse myself. I then move to someone else in the room.

Several weeks ago, I was at a cocktail party and overheard this conversation. The "interrogator", whose ancestors were obviously part of the Spanish Inquisition, was grilling a lovely woman on the recent separation from her husband. The questioner refused to drop the subject when it was so obviously disturbing to the woman...and the entire group.

"*You know your husband was sleeping around on you, don't you? Why did you put up with it so long?*" was actually one of the questions she posed.

Finally, the woman being interrogated stepped forward into the questioner's face and with a huge smile, quietly said:

"*Alright, I'm glad my separation is entertaining you but I'm finished with this. Excuse me while I go over and pick up one of those dessert forks and ram it into my left eye socket. I'd rather do that than stand here, condescending to interact with such a disdainful and insipid person.*"

What a wonderful cocktail party that was.

May I indulge you in a final few paragraphs on being asked uncomfortable questions? If you have children, I hope you are prepared for questions that will make you squirm, and blush. For the first four years of their existence, your children view you as the unarguable source of all information they require. During this stage, how you answer their questions will set the foundation of their lives. The manner in which you respond will either show them that their questions are important, or that they should not be asking questions, because you've made them feel it's wrong to be inquisitive.

Most questions asked to you by your children will be perfectly innocent, and at times you won't know the most factual answer.

The manner in which your child(ren) ask questions will tell you a lot about them. As the years pass you will see a definite pattern to their inquisitiveness that will give you an indication about both their IQ and EQ. You need to pay attention to this. **It's vital you know how to help your children unscramble all the data being bombarded at them. Encourage questions by asking your children questions. Let your children learn how to properly phrase a question, and how to position it logically.** Let them learn how to formulate answers early in their lives. Let them see how one well-placed question can open the door to a whole series of related questions.

I've always felt that having a quick answer is easy for most people. Speed of response does not guarantee accuracy of thinking. The real talent comes in having a truly great question. It's a scarce talent to find someone who can gather in information, mentally sort and file it, cut out the red herrings and as succinctly as is humanly possible, pose the most critical question in a simplistic and understandable manner. Do you do that yourself? Benjamin Franklin said, *"A question well asked is already half-answered."*

So with your children (and frankly with anyone) never shut down questions. I've actually heard parents chiding their children for asking too many questions and then directing them to sit quietly. How demoralizing for a young developing mind to be shut down so disrespectfully. As your children get older, the level of difficulty of their questions (both technically and emotionally) is going to increase multifold. You will be forced to rethink opinions that perhaps you haven't considered in decades...if at all. Your beliefs about religion, politics, sexual orientation, government, drugs, and family are going to be put to the test. For goodness sakes, don't imagine you can answer these off the cuff and don't try to answer before you and your mate have come to your own conclusions. I think it's crucial to go to children with a unified front in your responses, even if you disagree on the answer. It's perfectly sane to explain how one question can have many answers and opinions. *Mom and Dad don't always have to agree on everything, you know.*

For a little levity, here are actual questions asked of my wife and me by our two children. Their ages at the time are in the brackets following the question.

1. Daddy is there really a God or is he just made up for fun? (age 4)

2. Daddy, why is God so mean that he lets all these bad things happen to people? (age 6 referring to 9/11)

3. Daddy why do I have to go to school and do all this stupid homework when you are going to die and we're going to get all your money and your baseball card collection? (age 8)

4. Mommy, have you ever taken drugs? (age 11)

5. Dad, did you drink alcohol or smoke dope when you were my age? (age 12)

6. Dad, did you and Mom have sex before you were married? (age 14)

7. Mommy, what's a lesbiant? (age 7 and the way she said it)

8. Mommy, what's an f-ing homo? Am I a "f-ing" homo? My son actually said "f-ing" as I have written it. (age 4)

9. Daddy, kids in my Grade 7 class are having 'Rainbow Parties' (look it up) and the girls are giving the boys blowjobs. What's a blowjob? Does Mom give you blowjobs? (age 12)

10. Why are all the best athletes black? Where are the white guys? Don't they try as hard? (age 7)

If my kids actually deign to read this book, I guarantee that they are cringing right now. Their inquisitiveness was/is pure and deserves proper thinking and responses. We always did our best to be truthful and answer them as we would adults, not as mindless little beings. Talk down to children like they are children...and they will be remain children.

Two ideas that might help you when faced with questions that make you cringe. First, employ the "24 Hour Rule." Simply stated, difficult questions require some thoughtful consideration. You and your children agree that when a real heck of a question comes up, you have 24 hours to respond. It allows you to check how other parents (perhaps your own siblings) answered. You can go onto the Internet for background and information, or refer to the Parental Expert book you've got on the shelf. Oh yes, the parent asked the question must be the one to answer it.

A second idea is to offer your children the choice of asking the question verbally or in writing. Your response, at their choice, can be delivered in the same fashion. Sometimes it's easier to avoid embarrassment by asking the question "on a piece of paper."

Back to the onset of this Chapter, I would restate that there is really nothing truly wrong or indiscreet in a question when you consider the source. The true indiscretion will come if you answer it when you shouldn't, or in a careless manner.

Chapter 30 Key:

The only true indiscretion is in the answer, not the question. Don't ever be trapped into answering something you shouldn't.

Chapter 31

"The true measure of a man is how he treats someone who can do him absolutely no good..."

-Samuel Johnson 1709-1784

Giving back should be like breathing air...something that happens without thinking and doesn't stop until you die. When I was a kid attending our St. Mary's Catholic Church, I had difficulty with the concept of the collection plate. Every Sunday mass, older men in rumpled suits would walk down the aisles with a round wicker basket attached to a long pole. They would stand resolutely at the opening to the pew, and using the pole, would shove the basket in front of each person sitting there. I always wondered why the basket just wasn't passed hand to hand through the parishioners. I know that was a practice conducted in other churches. Perhaps the Catholic Church had experience with more money leaving the plate than being dropped into it. Perhaps they had learned the intimidation tactic of having that plate thrust in your face created the sense that God Himself was actually reaching out demanding alms. Either way, near the end of Mass, you were going to have a wicker basked thrust into your face.

I can remember being given 10 cents by my Mother at the beginning of each service. The dime was to be my contribution to the church. I just couldn't see how that one little dime was going to make a dent in the world of sorrows and woes the Priest was shouting at us... when he wasn't speaking mysteriously in Latin. Besides, that particular 10 cents in the 1960s would get you 20 blackballs or 15 gumballs. The sinful temptation to pocket the dime was often more than I could stand. I mastered the motion of reaching over the plate and not actually releasing my vice-like grip on that little coin. Secretively, it found its way into the safety of my left pocket, away from the prying eyes of my Mother. I look back at this with an element of entertainment, except for the fact that this philosophy and attitude towards "giving" unfortunately remained with me throughout the first four decades of my life.

As I got older, I gave a "respectable" donation to charities and then eagerly awaited the tax receipt...once a year. Most often I supported the United Way or the Cancer Society. If someone called at the door, I would cheerfully congratulate them on their spirit and efforts to collect, and confirm that I had already given. Walking down Toronto streets I would walk by street people with their caps, or empty Tim Horton cups in hand, asking for money. They wouldn't get a cent from me. I just could never accept that with a little effort they weren't able to find a job.

In 1996, the advertising agency where I worked was doing pro-bono advertising for the United Way of Greater Toronto. Soon after, I was invited to participate on the Board to help generate donations within the communications industry. I agreed to this, in part, because it seemed like a worth-while cause. I will admit that in the back of my Machiavellian mind, I also believed that joining the board would also build my resume and allow me to meet new contacts to further my career. Frightful wasn't it? That's how my mind operated in my hell-bent desire to drive my success. Anyway, at one of the United Way breakfast board meetings hosted by Manulife, a young mother of two was escorted to the podium to share a few words. She could have been 21 or 41 years old. I could not tell. She looked worse for wear and looked like a poster for the Shelters for Battered Women in Toronto. I can remember her vividly even today.

As a mother of a four year-old boy and a baby girl still in diapers, her story revealed that she existed in a living hell. Existed is the proper verb. She was hardly alive. Her cowardly excuse of a husband was a mean drunk who beat her mercilessly. She was not permitted to leave the apartment under any circumstance, at any time. She was not allowed to have anyone in the apartment with her. There was no telephone, radio or television. She was a prisoner with no contact to the outside world.

One night, after having brutally beaten his wife and physically assaulted the young lad, the man passed out in a drunken stupor. As he lay there on the kitchen floor, the woman grabbed the children, and with only the clothes they were wearing, ran out into the street. They must have looked a strange sight wandering helplessly through the dark.

Toronto's finest came along, and the two Police Officers helped her to a shelter where she found refuge. She told our group listening to her story, that the next few days were a blur...equally exhausting and terrifying. Every day she waited for her husband to hunt her down. Within a week, he did. He continued to hound her at the shelter until the Police officially intervened with a legal restraining order.

The people at the shelter counseled her professionally and compassionately. They had only her, and her children's best interests at heart. She had no money and no family in Canada to call on. She was alone except for her children...and the wonderful people at the shelter.

The young woman tenderly expressed her story clearly and without tears. She stood calmly in front of a room of industry captains who in their own right would have made any speaker nervous. It was easy to see how the circumstances of her life had decimated her confidence and virtually sucked the spirit of hope right out of her. Years of daily physical and emotional abuse had created a shell of a human being. Her inexpensive clothing was tidy and ironed. Her thin legs were bare and bruised. When asked about her children, her eyes sparkled and a wide smile appeared, momentarily camouflaging the bruises on her face. At no time did she appear angry, nor did she ask for money, or plead for help. She simply told her story. The audience was silent as we sat at our well-laid tables with linen table-cloths, crisply ironed napkins, $10.00 croissants and overpriced fruit trays. Her innocence and genuine honesty filled the air, and my heart.

I don't believe there was a dry eye in the entire room. With tears streaming down my cheeks and a lump in my throat, I stared incredulously at the woman. I wanted to hug her and tell her everything would be alright. I wanted to get her husband alone for five minutes in a dark alley. I was ashamed for my reasons for even being in the room. I felt embarrassed that I had been so thoughtless and uncaring. People like this woman needed help that I could have been giving throughout my life. Honestly, I even thought back to the number of times I had palmed that stupid dime rather that donate it to the wicker basket. I pledged to myself then and there that I would make a difference in how I gave of myself to others. Her story was my own personal kick in the behind. Giving was much more that just contemplating whether or not to put the 10 cents in a collection plate. It was an attitude shift that everyone needs to stop and realize that they can make a difference. In fact, they must make a difference. Not because others tell you to, or are watching. Not because it may further your career. You do it because **it's your duty as a human being to be humane and help others**. Every one of us can help financially and by donating our time to others. We don't have to wait for disasters of epic proportions. Every day in your very own city there are people starving, living on the streets, battling cancer or AIDS. The poor are getting poorer. Around the world children are dying every fifteen seconds due to water-related issues like drought and impurities. There is enough going on around you that you need to sit up, take notice and decide where to take a stand. *"The real heroes,"* said Nelson Mandella, *"Are the men and women who are friends of the poorest of the poor."*

Since that day in 1996, I have tried to do a much better job through donating money and time. The lady opened my eyes and I don't want them to ever close again. Find something to believe in, and invest your heart in it. I marvel at those superstars who have an endless well of generosity towards the less fortunate. They aren't necessarily financially wealthy but they are certainly wealthy in compassion and caring. These people obviously learned much earlier in life that did I, that helping others is not something we should even have to ponder. It's something that should be in all of our basic humanity to do.

Find something to believe in beyond yourself. How many friends and relatives have you lost to cancer? How many people do you know battling Alzheimer's or Parkinson's? How many people can you pass on the street without lending a helping hand? Give of yourself, no matter how little it is. Maya Angelou writes, *"I have found that among its other benefits, giving liberates the soul of the giver."* It certainly helps to liberate my soul.

I will close out this Chapter by telling you about two great Canadians who I have the pleasure of knowing. I don't wish to cause them any embarrassment by singling them out. It's just that their personal efforts towards others shine in my eyes. The first is Tony Gagliano who happens to be the Chairman and CEO of St. Joseph's Communications. Tony is a humanitarian extraordinaire and is the kind of example we all need to emulate. Tony has mastered the ability to fit 36 hours of time into every 24 hour day. A good part of that time is spent delivering against his philosophy, *"to serve a cause greater than our own self-interest." Tony.*" Tony oversees the St. Joseph Foundation to raise and allocate funds to the relief of poverty and the advancement of education. On top of running a highly successful company, Tony never takes his eye off his country, his community and as he phrases it, *"His given duty to give back to others in need."* Tony has justly received many accolades and awards for his service to the community and his country.

The second example I would share with you is John Cassaday who is the founding President and CEO of Corus Entertainment Inc. John's is the story of a really smart and decent person who has risen to the heights of the business world, while giving back to his community every step of the way. He sits on numerous boards and the list of business awards he has garnered, and company successes he has inspired, is too lengthy for me to type. My fingers would be aching afterwards.

I *will* share with you his "extra-curricular" activities like Chairing the United Way Campaign for Metro Toronto in 1995; and, Chairing the Board of St. Michael's Hospital from 2004-06. In 2004, John was the recipient of the Canadian Council of Christians and Jews Human Relations Award. Earlier in his career, he received the Paul Mulvihill Heart Award. How can one person be in so many places at one time and have the spirit to know the importance their personal sacrifice can have on others?

Like Tony Gagliano, John Cassaday discovered early in life the importance of giving. I can still hear the echo of John's words when he was my boss many decades ago. *"Howard, you do something because it is the right thing to do, not because it's going to make you look good."*

Both men are shining examples of making the conscious decision to get involved, do the right thing and make a difference. Both are highly successful in their respective careers. Both share in common a love of their family and an unwavering dedication to "giving back." **We are our brothers' keeper**.

Chapter 31 Key:

We <u>are</u> our brothers', and sisters' keepers. It is only right we help others by giving back of ourselves.

Chapter 32

"the massive in-roads in technology cannot overwhelm the burning need for an equally intense focus on generating and executing ideas..."

-Michael MacMillan

Follow along with me for a short story. Travel back in time with me and imagine it is a blistering hot and hazy Tuesday in the year 1508 A.D. Overhead, the bright blue Roman sky is devoid of any cloud cover. It's late morning and St. Peter's Square in the Vatican is saturated with people bustling about, discussing the events of the day, and trading their wares from their vendors' stalls. The sun is relentless as it pours down on you, the merchants, buyers and visitors making their pilgrimage to the Holiest of Churches in the Roman Catholic Empire.

In the centre of the square, the largest building towers above. The construction of St. Peter's Basilica won't begin for almost forty years, but the facades and statues surrounding the square are still very impressive, if not daunting. The most important office of the Vatican is located in the centre. On the second floor of that building is a sixty foot balcony from which his Holiness greets the crowd. The Pope will personally say the Sunday mass on special days. Today the windows on the balcony are open but immense purple velvet drapes have closed off the room from the intense heat, and the crowd below. If you look carefully at that window, you might espy a small head protruding from the right side of the curtain, observing the people below. Can you see it? Pope Julius II is watching his flock. Behind him in the candle-lit room are six Cardinals resplendent in their long flowing red robes. The learned men range in age from fifty to seventy-five. The eldest and most senior is Cardinal Veggianni-the Pope's most trusted advisor, and life-long best friend. Carefully studying the Pontiff, the Cardinal walks over to the draped window. He senses a great concern plaguing the Pope, like a dark cloud hanging over his friend's head.

"Excellency, are you pondering the moral suffering of your people?"

"No," the Pope answers quietly, after reflecting upon the question. "I am not pondering the moral suffering of my people."

"Then is it the Medici doctrine pertaining to the excommunication of those heretics in Florence? I know you've been contemplating that for several weeks now."

Pope Julius II turns away from the window and looks at his friend. He deliberately shakes his head signifying a negative response.

Veggianni continues to gently probe the issues of the day.

"I know what it is, Your Holiness. You are thinking on those *rumors* of the discovery of the WMD in the East. We're all concerned about that situation."

The Pontiff stiffens his shoulders and reacts immediately in a stern voice. "They aren't *rumors* about weapons of mass destruction. They are <u>factual</u> spy reports and I have it on good counsel from our allies that the Ottomans have all the necessary materials to build long range catapults. They have all the raw materials and the technology. We mustn't allow their firepower to out-match our friends?"

"No Excellency," the six Cardinals standing in the room answer in unison, all eyes on the floor. Obviously this is a touchy topic.

"Then it's the issue of the WMD that is upsetting your peace?" continues the elder Cardinal, carefully.

"No."

"What then is it my Pope? Something is obviously distressing you greatly. How may we help?"

The Pontiff walks away from the window and steps slowly over to his large desk. It is littered with books and parchments. The room silently awaits the words and wisdom of the leader of the Roman Catholic Church,

God's representative on Earth. His brow is furrowed and he reaches up his right hand to rub his temples.

"It's the price of paint," the Pope finally admits.

"The p-price of p-p-paint?" one of the Cardinals asks meekly, stuttering the words.

"Yes, the price of all the paint that Michelangelo has requisitioned for his work on the Sistine Chapel," Pope Julius II clarifies, anger underlying and punctuating each word. "He's going to bankrupt me. Doesn't he understand that we have budgets and timelines to meet?"

One of the younger men, a very ambitious Cardinal Tassonni steps forward and humbly enters the conversation.

"Your Holiness, I have met with the great artist several times. His vision for the Chapel is extraordinary. His thoughts seem to have been given him and ordained by God Himself. He isn't called *"Il Divino"* for nothing. What's the price of paint going to matter in a thousand years when good Christians from around the world come to the Vatican to view the Chapel?"

Pope Julius II's face reddens as he straightens himself out to his full height of 5'6".

"What's the price of paint got to do with it? A thousand years from now? Are you not thinking clearly Tassonni? I asked for a simple painting on a wall. *Give me the twelve Apostles and a nice background* were my exact words to him. Raphael was there directly standing beside me and heard the entire briefing word for word. I could not have been clearer. Three weeks was the deadline and *"Il Divino"* as you call him, had four assistants to mix the paints and hold up the six oil lanterns." The Pope started scratching at his balding scalp before continuing his tirade.

"And where are we today? The "artist" believes we should be using the Chapel walls and ceiling to depict the Creation, the Downfall of Man and the Promise of Salvation. He's planning over three hundred figures and yesterday told me that he's adding in a section on Adam and Eve, The Garden of Eden and The Great Flood. Where do creative people come up with all of this? *"What about my 3 weeks?"* I asked him. He simply shrugged his shoulders and mumbled something about my legacy and that the Chapel would not be ready for at least another 3 years. 3 years! He has employed sixty assistants, requires two hundred oil lanterns and two vats of premium oil. He's going to have our books in the red. I should have known better. Two years ago I commissioned *this same Michelangelo* to build my tomb and it is still not completed. How long does it take to build a tomb? I can't wait 3 years for the Sistine Chapel. We need to get this completed in *real time."*

The Cardinals shift uneasily in their sandals. None of them, including Veggianni have ever seen the Pope rant on so angrily. He is usually very calm and peaceful.

"His vision and ideas do sound magnificent," counters Veggianni respectfully. "We do have a full treasury and if we were ever going to make an investment, this might be the time."

The Pontiff walks towards his oldest friend and places a gentle hand on his left shoulder. He speaks very slowly.

"I agree that it does sound marvelous, but what good is it to me if it's not done while I'm still alive? I invest all the money for a decent idea and my successor will get the credit. I'm the one stuck with the accountants and the foolishness of those two moronic Senators, Sarbannius and Oxleyionis crying foul every time we try to make our numbers come together. The Church has financial obligations. Employees like Michelangelo could bankrupt this entire organization."

"Bankrupt the Catholic Church. Heavens no," the Cardinals cry out in a chorus. "The Church will never be bankrupt." Everyone in the room quickly makes the sign of the cross and looks up towards the Heavens. The Pope offers a blessing and then re-directs his questions.

"Alright then, so what do we do? We have all this modern technology and yet we are being held up to ransom by some *idea man* who doesn't understand the price of labor, scaffolds and lantern oil. Doesn't he follow the price of oil? Who does he think he is...*Leonardo Da Vinci?* Let's brainstorm and have some ideas. Who is first?"

One by one the Cardinals proffer suggestions. A bald, incredibly over-weight scribe enters the room and begins writing frantically on a scroll. The loud scratching of his writing implement on the parchment is intrusive and the Pope shoots him a glance of annoyance.

Veggianni begins. "Excellency, you are right. It appears we are not using our technology to the utmost. A completion date of another two to three years is unacceptable. I suggest that we employ our modern architectural system of cranes and levers to dismantle the Chapel: remove the roof and lower it to the ground. That would eliminate the need for all of the scaffolding and this foolishness of Michelangelo laying down on his back and painting upwards."

Tassonni quickly jumps in. "That's a brilliant idea Veggianni. It would cut out all the cost of the scaffolding. Michelangelo could paint using the sunlight and that would eliminate the lanterns, the 2 vats of lantern oil and all the staff he hired on last week. This would save us a fortune. We'll terminate his staff immediately and give them an extra bag of salt or two to tide them over until they get new jobs.'"

Pope Julius II smiles and gently nods. "Those are wonderful suggestions gentlemen and they show me you understand the gravity of the situation. What else can we do?"

Two middle-aged Cardinals raise their hands and speak in a back and forth fashion.

"Highness, we could use our new spray paint technology to at least do the background skies and clouds. It's only going to be some blue and white paint which we could import at a reduced cost from the Greek island of Santorini. Painting the sky and clouds isn't exactly chariot science. We've been discussing this and would wager two pieces of silver this shortcut would eliminate 40% of the time required."

The room is thrown into silence as the Pope and the remaining Cardinals glare at the duo...mouths agape. The two Cardinals immediately recognize their gaffe. Gambling is considered a sin in the Catholic Church.

"Just a figure of speech, Your Holiness," one on them pipes up immediately as the two Cardinals take a step backwards, their eyes locking on the robes of the Pope to avoid his disappointed look.

Tassonni, seeing the chance to interrupt the awkward silence and re-focus the meeting offers, "Your Excellency. We could use instant messaging to keep you better informed and involved in the progress of the Chapel. It's not right that your time is wasted in meetings and travel to and fro. You're far too busy for that.

The Pope nods his agreement and motions for the Cardinal to continue this subject of instant messaging.

"We'll have a second, much less accomplished, or costly artist stand beside Michelangelo and charcoal-sketch his progress. Every hour we can have this "shadow" artist send his updates to us by C-p-mail. More often if you require. You can simply monitor the progress and send back your comments or suggestions. Think of the costs and time we'll save using the C-p-mail."

The Pope turns to Veggianni and whispers, "C-p-mail?"

"Carrier pigeon mail, Your Holiness," the Cardinal whispers in reply. "It's the latest business craze. Saves time like you can't imagine... except of course in really bad thunderstorms when the system goes down because the birds can't fly. Then there is no guarantee of same day delivery."

"Good idea," the Pontiff speaks aloud to the room. "C-p-mail."

All the Cardinals smile and murmur assent. The sound of the scribe scribbling frantically on the stiff parchment now seems less of an annoyance.

"Ah, instant messaging and C-p-mail," the Holy Men in the room murmur quietly.

Veggianni is impressed with the diplomatic skill that Tassonni is displaying during the meeting. The younger Cardinal is customarily much less tactful. He smiles at the younger Cardinal who blushes with the sin of pride.

To the side of the group a tall, very thin Cardinal looks uncomfortable. His long red robes seem to have been fashioned for a much shorter man. Cardinal Vittorio Peritti lowers his head and clears his throat. The other men turn to look at him. The man is known to have an incredibly sharp mind albeit masked in a cloud of insecurity.

"Do you have something to add, Peritti?" the Pope acknowledges the interruption and asks patiently.

"Perhaps I do, Holiness."

"Then go on and share your thinking."

"Well Excellency, if we are certain that all of this new technology is not going to damage the integrity of Michelangelo's creativity and his ideas, then I do have a suggestion."

"What is it?" Veggianni asks encouragingly.

"Digitali Replicanus," the tall Cardinal begins. "We can save considerable time and cost if we cut the number of Michelangelo's painted figures from his estimate of 300 to 30. We will instruct him to personally paint only 10 of the 30 figures and have two much less expensive apprentices copy each of the Master's figures twice. I have seen this "digitali replicanus" technology and have witnessed the benefits."

"I love it," joined Tassonni. "No one looks really carefully at all the faces on a wall mural, and who is going to strain their necks looking up at the top of a ceiling. I know I wouldn't. Perhaps we even make it a little harder to see the faces by cutting back the lighting in the Chapel."

"Another cost saving," Peritti smiles. "Praise Be."

Pope Julius II looks over at his shy Cardinal. "Excellent suggestion my friend, and let me reassure you. I can't really see how being a little cost and time prudent can actually hurt what Michelangelo is doing."

The room falls silent for heartbeats as the Cardinals gather around the scribe and read his notes. There are excellent suggestions neatly documented on the parchment. The mood of the room has lightened and they exchange smiles. They look over to the Pontiff and see his shoulders finally relaxing beneath his heavy garments. They take comfort as he exhales loudly.

"My children," he begins, "Let us pray."

All in the room bow their heads. The scribe puts down his writing implement and kneels on the floor. In the presence of such experienced and wise men he is humbled...and yet perplexed.

Musing, the scribe asks himself, "Have they missed the entire point? Of course the artist's work and ideas will be compromised. People will look at the faces on the walls and the ceiling. When they see the duplication it can't but help but negatively affect how they think about the artist, the Pope and the Church. Learning that Michelangelo lay on his back to complete this masterpiece is a story that will travel the entire earth for centuries to come. His great work will be a monument to God and to man's excellence. Is this only about saving money and time?" He silences his mind as Pope Julius II begins to pray.

"Dear Lord who guides us in our every action. Thank you for the wisdom of my Cardinals. Their thinking will overcome the vanity and careless wastage of your servant Michelangelo. You have shown us the technological ideals to complete a very simple task with a minimum of effort, time and cost. Please continue to guide us to develop even more superior technology to achieve our goals. Amen."

The end of the prayer signals that the meeting is over. The Cardinals take turns bowing and reverently kissing the immense ruby ring on the Pope's left hand. After receiving an individual blessing, each man files silently from the room. Only Cardinal Veggianni remains. Pope Julius II returns to his original position beside the draped window and looks outside.

"The crowd is thinning in the noon-day heat," he observes, after pulling back an edge of the drape.

Veggianni stands behind him and looks down into the square.

"So Veggianni," the Pope says, over his shoulder. "Do you think we've fixed this arrogant Michelangelo so that we can save on his costs and get the Chapel completed in two months? Or will this Sistine Chapel project linger on for years to come like his construction of my tomb?"

"Definitely two months, Your Excellency," the Cardinal says very reassuringly. "I have no doubt."

"I'm not so sure," Pope Julius II counters as a tiny smile crosses his lips. "Care to put a wager on it?"

———————————

Alright, now come back present day time. Obviously this story is revisionist history. It is fact that Pope Julius II did commission Michelangelo to construct both his tomb and to paint the Sistine Chapel. It is also fact that the original briefing was completely discarded when Michelangelo brought forward his vision of the entire Chapel, including the famous ceiling. The completion of both the Pope's tomb and the Sistine Chapel far exceeded all timelines. The latter wasn't completed for four years. If you've been to Rome and Vatican City, I trust you went to view the Chapel. It is one of the most magnificent works of art you will ever encounter. If you have not seen it, plan to.

My story is an exaggeration of the point that people and companies are so enamored with the physical technology of our inventions, and so hamstrung by their short-term budget planning, they are not keeping up with the ideas being fed into, and through the new technologies. It seems to be more important to discuss the capital expenditures on new computers, programming and hand-held devices than it is to discuss the investment in the brainpower and thinking needed to bring those devices and technology to life.

Without well-conceived and crafted ideas, the upgrades in our technology will mean nothing. It will be like manufacturing a beautifully sleek 80 foot schooner...without any wind for its sails. It will be the construction of a 22nd Century shuttle-craft rocketing to Mars...without any fuel or oxygen. Ideas take the courage of both the individual creating them, and the company opening its mind and structures to welcome them. Ideas need people who aren't afraid to be told "no" five times before having their great idea to fight its way to the surface. Successful ideation takes people looking out ahead of the masses and trends that have already hit the street. How has Madonna managed to capture three distinctive generations of fans across a hundred nationalities?

Creativity can't survive where there is constant cost cutting driven by analysts telling organizations what to do. Don't think me naïve, but companies must exist beyond margins. The short-term vision that complements current CEO remuneration models is crippling to the North American economy.

How are you personally balancing your focus on understanding and keeping up with technological advances versus generating new ideas and thinking to complement them? What is happening in your company to encourage new ideas and thinking? **Not every idea generated has**

to be a home run. Babe Ruth struck out no less than three times for every home run he ever hit. Singles and doubles can be a very effective tactic to win the game. The CEO of Corus, John Cassaday recently told an audience, *"Don't get blindsided into thinking your idea has to be the next I-Pod."*

Allow me to leave you with one thought for all those times you are feeling that your great thinking is being subjugated. Roger Shank, author of *"The Creative Attitude"* wrote that:

"Many people will react to your new and different ideas and explanations by saying NO and by asserting that things are not your way, but their way. Don't let them force you into abandoning your ideas, but instead follow your ideas through and submit them to your own tests and assumptions and see what they will bear."

Here are some of my favorite quotes regarding potential new ideas. Note the initial reaction to what we now know to be incredible successes. How many ideas were rejected because of short-sightedness and/or a lack of persistence of the person behind the idea? How many of your ideas were rejected that you should be resurrecting? Read a few of these quotes I pulled off *"Businessballs.com"*:

"But what is it good for?" --Senior engineer at the Advance Computing Systems Division of IBM, 1968, commenting on the microchip.

"There is no reason anyone would want a computer in their home." --Ken Olson, Chairman and Founder of Digital Equipment Corp., 1977.

"Who the hell wants to hear actors talk?" --H.M. Warner Brothers, 1927.

"A cookie store is a bad idea. Besides, the market research reports say America likes crispy cookies, not soft and chewy cookies like you make." --rejection to Debbie Fields' idea of starting Mrs. Fields' Cookies.

"We don't like their sound, and guitar music is on the way out." --Decca Recording rejecting the Beatles, 1962.

"*Airplanes are interesting toys but of no military value.*" -- Marechal Ferdinand Foch, Professor of Strategy, Ecole Superieure de Guerre.

"*Louis Pasteur's theory of germs is ridiculous fiction.*" –Pierre Pachet, Professor of Physiology at Toulouse, 1872.

"*Everything that can be invented has been invented.*" --Charles H. Duell, Commissioner of U.S. Office of Patents, 1899.

Chapter 32 Key:

Technology is a two-headed creature. To keep it optimally working for humanity it must be constantly fed great thinking and ideas. When the feeding stops, the beast will turn on us. We must have courage and foresight to embrace new ideas and thinking. Don't let small-minded people reject your great ideas. Persist in bringing them to life.

Chapter 33

"Do or do not. There is no try..."

-Yoda in *The Empire Strikes Back*

We all need heroes in our lives. My first heroes came to me through a large movie screen at our local movie theatre. Some of my most memorable lessons in life have come from those movies I have watched and re-watched throughout my life. Sitting there in the dark of the theatre, I was enraptured with the basic good guy versus bad guy scenarios. With a little suspended disbelief I was always patiently thrilled to see the protagonist come out on top. My best lessons were taught to me by John Wayne, Gary Cooper, Jimmy Stewart and a raft of actors I grew to love and emulate. How many movies did John Wayne show us how a man was supposed to behave and look? He was an equally smart hero whether he was a cowboy or a marine. Duke was tough as nails and always driven to a mission of success. Rooster Cogburn in *True Grit* single-handedly taking on Ned Pepper and his outlaw crew. Then there was Jimmy Stewart as a fledgling senator in *Mr. Smith Goes to Washington* taking on a corrupt mob boss. Gary Cooper was Will Kane in *High Noon,* and no amount of fear or pressure from his Quaker wife played by Grace Kelly, would make him turn tail and run. I learned to adore the amazingly crafted movies directed by David Lean, Frank Capra, Billy Wilder and Martin Scorsese. They were (and are) master story tellers who could capture your imagination through their film and deeply embed in your psyche a message that challenged you to think about yourself and life.

Sadly, my love of movies has waned over the past decade. I no longer consider myself a movie trivia expert because the dramatic shift in the caliber of recent movies, and the methodology of those stories being told. Digital effects have taken away from my imagination's ability to interact with the big screen. Story-lines are confused and often absurd. **When I was growing up in theatres, the good guys wore white hats and the bad guys all looked like evil. They were easy to pick out with stubble, a dangling cigarette, slicked-back hair and a sneer.** Now, antagonists seem to come out on the winning end of the stick as often as the good guy. The lines between evil and good aren't crystal clear. There's a lot left for interpretation and too much suspended disbelief and CGI for my liking.

But movies and your heroes change with time and maturity. Soon you start to look to the real world. My transition from movie heroes to real life began with a Canadian politician who made me stop and think about my role and duty to Canada. In either of our two languages, he would eloquently converse with anyone about anything. Although he was the public figure to be interviewed, he enjoyed countering reporters with questions, as well as answering them. This politician was Pierre Trudeau. He was our Canadian Prime Minister from 1968-79 and then again from 1980-1984. What immediately endeared him to me was that he didn't shirk away from making the most crucial decisions that were needed. As a true leader, he surrounded himself with outstanding minds. He used these minds to input but once decided he was resolute to the end. When the Font du Liberation du Quebec (FLQ) unleashed their terrorist actions on the country in 1968, the country was thrust into a state of shock and panic. The media was in a feeding frenzy. There was an ominous mood across every recess of the nation. The world stage focused its cameras and attention on Canada.

Calmly appearing before the nation, Trudeau explained exactly what had transpired. He spoke with confidence and conviction. In very simple phrases, he outlined why it was necessary to execute a very stringent policy called *The War Measures' Act*. This Act would station soldiers into the nation's capital of Ottawa to counter what appeared to be an obvious vulnerability to the terrorists. It would permit the authorities to detain anyone without arresting them. It was to be enacted instantly and of course, within all limits of the law. The media jumped on the civil rights bandwagon and tried to stir national and global opinion against the government. Trudeau to his credit did not back down. He wouldn't bend to any media-driven public outcry. When asked on the steps of Parliament if he would respond to the terrorists in the same fashion that they were conducting themselves, he smiled, and stated his famous quote, *"Just watch me."* And the world did.

The FLQ was corralled and our Prime Minister gained instantaneous recognition as a leader to be reckoned with. Throughout his tenure of placing Canada on the world stage, Pierre Trudeau made us think about our country, our Canadian Charter of Rights, bilingualism, federalism and patriotism. He never succumbed to the usual pressure imparted to the Prime Minister by the President of the United States. Under his watch, we would not become, or act like, the 51st State. He approached his job with a global eye and perspective. Canadians had to struggle to keep up to his keen intellect and gregarious spirit.

I'm sure there are many detractors to this man's legacy but no one can argue that under his guidance, Canada became a greater nation.

My second true to life hero is a young boy whose spirit and cross country trek captured the world's imagination and heart. Terry Fox lost most of his right leg to bone cancer in 1977 at the age of 18. The long term prognosis was not good. I first read in the newspaper about some teen-age kid who was going to run across Canada to raise money for cancer. That in its own right was pretty cool. Then I discovered the teen-age kid only had one leg. I watched on the evening news as this Terry Fox guy dipped his artificial leg into the Atlantic Ocean at St. John's Newfoundland. He turned and shyly smiled for the camera. He hobbled back from the water's edge and began to run: Prosthetic limb and all. What he was doing looked painful as hell. In my own estimation, I gave him a week before he quit. No one could run on a fake leg for more than a few days.

The first week passed and he was still running. Then the second and third weeks flew by. Every night there would be a brief film on this one-legged kid running along the side of a highway. How could your admiration not grow?

"What city is he in today?" everyone would ask, as Terry became a topic of daily conversation.

Terry entered Toronto and loped into Nathan Phillips' Square. Faceless, I stood there in the mob watching him make his way up to the podium. He wasn't very big in stature and he looked just like everyone else from where I stood. His curly hair was matted with sweat and he seemed uncomfortable being the centre of attention from so many people. He looked up and a warm smile appeared on his face. My heart pounded with joy. Terry spoke quietly and the crowd exploded with his every comment. Tears ran down my cheeks. The euphoric atmosphere he created that day was something I had never experienced. He left the stage, shook a few hands and in no time was making his way out of Toronto. I watched for news of him every day and read the newspapers.

Then disaster happened. Terry was approaching Thunder Bay when he was hospitalized. It had never occurred to me that he wasn't going to be absolutely fine, leave the hospital, finish the run, dip his artificial leg in the Pacific, and go back to school. My optimism was foolish and short-lived.

The rest you know. Terry Fox succumbed to cancer in June, 1981. It was a very dark time. He had unintentionally touched millions of Canadians and had lit a national torch that had never been seen before. I don't think I really felt much about anything, or anyone for a long time after that. W.H. Auden wrote that, *"No hero is immortal until he dies."* Auden was wrong. Terry Fox was already an immortal long before that.

The young teenager had run 5373 kilometers in 143 days. To put that in perspective, that's 26 miles (only 0.2 less than a complete marathon) every day, seven days a week for 143 days. Since Terry's death, the foundation named to honor him has raised well over $400 million towards the battle against cancer. When I seriously took up running in 2005, I kept track of my own mileage in a running log book. I started plotting my daily mileage on a map of Canada so I could measure the distance I had covered. I began my own trek in Vancouver, and then ran east through the Rockies and across the Prairies. It took most of my first full year of running to arrive in Northern Ontario. I notched up enough miles to make it to Thunder Bay where in my imagination, I met my hero. He was healthy and cancer-free. I stood there with Terry and shook his hand, and we shared a laugh. We put on our running shoes and headed out for a run. In my dream, Terry Fox was running along-side me--both his legs intact: A wonderful grin on his freckled face and the sun on his brow. **Isn't this what a hero is supposed to be about? Isn't it someone to show you the way; lead by example; tackle an almost impossible feat; charge a windmill; and, inspire us to be better?**

Who will my son look up to as his heroes? Me? I certainly hope so. Right now I fear that his heroes would gravitate towards Stewie and Peter Griffen of The Family Guy. Kevin Garnett of the Celtics? Sidney Crosby of the Penguins. Bart and Homer Simpson. Kratos-God of War? Simon Cowell of American Idol? It might be Halo, or Robot Chicken. Are there true heroes out there that my son and all of our children will want to honor and emulate?

We need to help the next generation understand the importance of role models and heroes. They shouldn't just look up to the grossly overpaid professional athletes; the all-too-quick movie "stars"; or, the rock performers who don't seem to realize that they provide role models for a million set of eyes and impressionable minds. **Our world needs heroes.** I'm certain there are people in your world who consider you a hero. I'm sure there are people who watch you closely so they can learn. Keep that in mind with your every action, every day. Try not to pull an Eliot Spitzer on the people who adore you.

Where is John Wayne when we need him?

Chapter 33 Key:

We all need heroes to help show us the way. You be a hero to someone and try never to get knocked off the pedestal.

Chapter 34

"Story-telling is the most powerful way to put ideas into the world today..."

-Robert McAfee Brown

Everyone has a story to tell, if you only give them a chance to tell it. My mother had many wonderful talents and qualities: None more pronounced than her ability to tell a story, and in return, have someone tell her their story. In fact, I always felt my mother, if given the chance, could talk the eyes off a snake. The reality is that Mom was raised the youngest of four daughters on a very remote farm. Aside from farm chores and school, there wasn't a lot to do...but talk.

I grew up watching my mother and her sisters visiting each other. They could conduct a lively conversation for hours on end. It wasn't the stuff that gossip is made of. It was stories about people with whom they had grown up. After a lengthy visit, and chat, everyone would disperse to their respective homes. Within minutes, our phone would ring and it would be one of the aunts calling to catch up with Mom. It was incredible. They had just been "catching up" for the last three hours. What in the world could they still find to talk about?

My friends loved coming to our house and I'm certain it was to sit and talk with Mom. Even when I was off at university or living in Toronto, my friends would drop in for a visit with my parents. One friend told me that my mother could get him talking about things he didn't even share with his own family.

"One talk with your mother is like a month of therapy," a pal told me. *"I find she brings out stories in me I hadn't realized were all that important."*

Age was of no consideration when Mom was talking to someone. She treated older people with amazing respect and would listen for hours to stories from their younger years. Similarly, I watched her talk with children of all ages, always managing to encourage a good exchange with even the shyest of personalities.

Maya Angelou said,

"There is no greater agony that bearing an untold story inside of you."

I think Maya Angelou would have loved my mother who instinctively knew this statement to be true. Mom often said that she believed everyone, especially older people and children, had incredible stories to tell. Ironically, these are the two groups of people that the world doesn't seem all that interested in listening to. Certainly the world wants to make money from their needs. They just don't want to unlock their stories.

My mother was also blind to skin color. I've mentioned that I was raised in a very small city in Ontario. In my early years, the population was almost 100% Caucasian. We were not ethnically diverse and I would politely impose the term "redneck" on a lot of people I knew. The only diversity in our city was in the ethnically slandering jokes that were rampant. In the 1960s this began to change as a great number of people of different ethnicities moved to the city. It was a new, if not unsettling, beginning for a very small, old-fashioned town set in its ways.

One evening after dinner, there was a knock at our front screen door. It had to be a stranger because any relatives or neighbors would do a quick knock and immediately enter. A man was standing on our porch and he asked us if we had anything to sell. He was in his late 20s, not tall, not short, and had a very pleasing smile. He was a foreigner to us and his skin was brown. He spoke with a thick accent and he appeared nervous. In a moment, my mother came to the door and without hesitation opened it. She smiled at the stranger, and noting the sweat on his brow, offered a glass of water. Mom didn't wait for a response but gave me a glance which told me "hop to it."

"Are you new to the city?" Mom asked the stranger.

"Yes Ma'am," he replied, with a thick accent.

"Welcome," Mom said cheerfully. "Are you starting a new business?"

"Yes Ma'am. I'm going to open a used goods store with furniture and house-hold items. I'm going to buy items and then sell them on consignment for people. "

The stranger's ability to comfortably speak English was very limited and he struggled to find the word "consignment."

"Well that sounds terrific. How's it going so far?" Mom asked, clearly enunciating each word and slowing down her speech. This caught my attention and I realized how kind she was being to someone we didn't even know.

The man shook his head and frowned. He took a long drink from the glass of water.

"Not so good Ma'am," he answered honestly. "No one will talk with me or sell me their goods. I feel like a leper."

My mother asked the man inside where it was cooler. The two stood by the door and talked for the next twenty minutes. I heard Mom ask about his wife, children and home in India. He was a very formal man but in a few minutes he was laughing, and despite his struggles with the language, was holding his own. The man came to life telling his story. Mom told him about her farm and how travelling salesmen would often come to the door looking for items to buy or sell. Her mother would always make time for them and offer them her welcome. Mom asked him where he was considering setting up his store and then suggested a number of locations he might look into.

My father was sitting at the kitchen table, observing the whole visit. He didn't involve himself but watched with curiosity. He certainly sat up when Mom invited the stranger to look throughout our house for items he might wish to buy and then re-sell at his store. Within a few minutes, four to five items were agreed to and the man wrote out a receipt documenting the date, the items, the agreed-to value and his signature. The only issue appeared to be that the man didn't have any money and couldn't pay for the items until after they were sold...thus the word "consignment." The man very congenially smiled, warmly thanked my mother and left.

My mother took a great deal of flak and razzing about the entire episode. Jokes were told at the stranger's expense, and the commonly-held opinion was that we would never see a cent from any of the items. Mom took it all in and held her ground.

"He'll be back," she stated firmly. "Just wait and see."

Three weeks later, we learned that a new store had opened up on the edge of the downtown core. It was a "new and used items" store and was being run by "foreigners." The whole concept didn't sit well with the general populace. Mom and Dad immediately paid the new store a visit. Mom clarified that it was not to "check on her items." Rather, it was to wish the new owners Good Luck. When they arrived at the store, my parents were greeted like royalty. Everyone working at the store was related to the man who had made the deal with Mom. Within minutes the conversations were in full flight.

Several weeks later, there was a knock at our front door. The store owner, no longer a stranger to us, was standing on our porch. I answered the door and the man, grinning from ear to ear, handed Mom an envelope.

"As agreed to," he stated proudly, as Mom took the envelope. "You should count it."

Mom took the envelope and placed it inside one of the many pockets on her apron. She smiled warmly and said, "No need for that. How's business?"

"It has really picked up," the man said. "I now have carpets and hundreds of items for sale. Come to the store and I will give you a great deal."

I noticed his English was better and he appeared more confident and relaxed. I had a feeling his *leprosy* was less contagious. He and Mom spoke about his family, and again I watched her disarm the stranger with questions about his past and his dreams for the store. After a few minutes the man turned to leave.

"I will not forget you Mrs. Breen," he spoke quietly. "You trusted a complete stranger when most people here were closing the door in my face."

As the years passed, the little store grew steadily and after a decade it was one of the largest resellers of carpeting and flooring in the entire county. My parents were steady customers and with every visit were reminded that they had been "the first." I remember asking Mom why she had trusted a total stranger. She reflected for a moment and then said, "*He looked like a decent man. Besides, he told a really good story about his wife, children and his home. He just needed to be given the chance to talk about what was important.*"

The art of story-telling is waning. **Our histories, and the lessons they hold, seem to be of less importance with each passing generation.** Our desire, or perhaps our curiosity to have a deep conversation with another person, isn't as strong as it used to be. Opening ourselves to a conversation with a stranger, or someone "different", isn't common-place. We hold our privacy close to our chest, perhaps out of fear, prejudice, or just a lack of social graces. I think there are other factors involved in our lack of ability in both telling stories and encouraging others to tell stories.

1. **Our generation is losing its respect for "words"…both written and verbal.** Today's population has lost the richness and depth of the words available to be used. The art of describing something with wonderfully adept and colorful adjectives seems to be a thing of the past. Short forms and acronyms have replaced real words. Conversations now live on e-mail and text messages where economy of words used is vital for speed. Verbal conversations with people under 30 sound like clipped recaps on the news rather than intelligent conversations.

2. Listen to lyrics of **modern music** which use **expletives** as descriptive adjectives more often than naught. **DVDs**, reality television programming, **verbally abusive** cooking shows, **graphically violent** computer and video games and music where the words "bitch and whore" used to describe young girls are simply the norm.

3. I've loved the Harry Potter series of books and I'm encouraged that J.K. Rowling helped re-indoctrinate an entire generation of new readers. My concern is how these books and J.R.R. Tolkien's masterpieces were taken into movie format with such amazingly wonderfully computer-generated visuals that so much of our imaginations rendered inadequate. **How can my imagination**

compete against the computer graphics of today's movies?

4. **We are guilty of not telling our children stories.** We're allowing our exhaustion and time pressures to be excuses for giving our children endless time with computer games and videos. We all need to find the time with our kids to share stories from our younger years, as well as stories from our parents' youth. What might seem boring and dull to you will be of interest to your kids. We all want to learn more about our personal history and from whence we've come. It takes effort and a commitment of time on your behalf. **By telling the stories, you'll help to foster a sense of communication with your children.** The more descriptive you make your stories, the more they will learn to expand their vocabulary. The more curious they may become to want learn more. I can only hope that with your effort and example, it might open up a venue for your children to want to share their own stories with you and others.

I make it a practice now to try to unlock stories from strangers. I take one moment to ask a simple question, *"How's your family today?"* It's amazing how this simple opener will get people to talk. Don't accept the answer, *"Fine, thank-you."* Continue with, *"How many children do you have?"* That always does the trick. People want to talk. They want to connect on some level. Asking the girl behind the Tim Hortons' counter about her day doesn't make you beholding to her. There won't be a backlash for trying to be polite.

I spend a lot of time in cabs and airport lounges. Rather than sit like a lump on a log, I spark up a conversation whenever I can. Why should we sit in silence? Do you know that I've learned more in cabs and airport lounges, than in almost any other places? Here are three items that arose from talking with strangers. I financially benefitted from them all:

1. **EBay:** During early September, 1998 it seemed that every conversation I had with a taxi driver ended with a discussion of the "buzz" about this new on-line company going public before Oct. 1st. I can thank 5-6 cab drivers for sparking my interest and getting me involved when E-Bay went public on September 21/98.

2. **Rim:** In 1997, I was sitting in an airport lounge in San Francisco when I struck up a conversation with a fellow traveler. Our plane to Toronto was delayed and we had two hours to kill. He reached into his briefcase and pulled out a really cool hand-held device. It was the forerunner to the Blackberry and it looked incredible. My hand-held device, touted as providing immediate wireless e-mail, was a waste of time. As I looked at this new black device the man described it as his "crackberry" and admitted to being an addict. When I arrived back in Toronto, I instantly began looking at investing in RIM and was thrilled when it went public in January 1998.

3. **The price of gold:** When my family was travelling in Greece last year we found ourselves in a cab being driven by a man who had been a teacher in Chicago. He was very out-spoken and didn't need much encouragement to share his story. After telling us about his family, his favorite meals to cook and teaching in Chicago, he mentioned the affect the strong Euro was having on Greece. He was very concerned about inflation and the rising price of oil. The rising price of oil would raise his gas prices, lower his profits and raise the cost to buy fresh vegetables. It was then he said something that sparked me. He mentioned that despite the Euro, he knew that if the price of oil continued to rise, and the middle-East continued to be in "disarray," that the price of Gold was going to rise dramatically. He mentioned this in a very nonchalant manner and it was a blinding glimpse of the obvious that I had been ignoring. So much for all my financial training, planning and wizardry. It took a 72 year-old Greek cab driver to re-focus my attention on the bigger picture. For those of you not following Gold, the price has more than doubled in the past 16 months.

Chapter 34 Key:

Don't let storytelling die. Be curious and respectful in helping other people share their story with you. Be prepared to share your stories with your children and others. You will benefit from this many times over. Everyone has a story to tell if given half a chance.

Chapter 35

"Society never advances. It recedes as fast on one side as it gains on the other. Society acquires new arts, and loses old instincts..."

-Ralph Waldo Emerson

We have become a "porch-less society." Despite the sky being filled with dark grey thunderheads, my son Christian and I took our dog Ginger for a walk the other night. We weren't far from home when the clouds unleashed and it began to viciously pour. We raced back to our house and stood at the front door looking up at the ominous sky, watching the rain as it pounded on our neighbors' houses and cars. The ensuing lightening show was terrific and the thunder made the earth shudder.

Standing there with my boy, I reminisced about the earlier years of my youth, and the street upon which I was raised. I have fond memories of sitting on our front porch watching and listening to thunderstorms. Neighbors would come out of their house and sit on their front porch to take in the spectacle. Kids would run back and forth across the street from porch to porch...visiting for a moment or two with their friends. As lightening took over the sky, people would exclaim astonishment and count down until the thunder would sound. Neighbors and friends would call across the street to exchange reactions. I loved sitting on our porch during storms, especially when my whole family was there. Mom would tell stories about her youth on the farm and explain how a bad storm could really cause damage to the fields, and the barn.

Today, an entire generation doesn't know that people had porches at the **front** of their houses. These porches served a purpose far beyond watching the rain or providing a different aesthetic to the front of your house. After dinner, it was the habit to sit outside on your front porch. It was customary to visit your neighbors' porches or, to be visited. Perhaps, it was because there was no air-conditioning inside the house, and the summer heat drove people outside. Perhaps, it was a more neighborly time when people were genuinely interested in catching up on the news of the street. The connectivity we knew and experienced was face to face and daily. The porches were our "chat rooms."

We don't have porches at the front of our houses anymore. People have migrated to the rear of their house to sit on their patio, or their deck. Tall fences in our backyards separate us from our neighbors to protect our "privacy." We don't watch our kids play on the street because it's safer for them to play in the backyard, or to be dropped off at a playgroup. Societal changes have driven us from our front porch to our back yard, and now inside our house to our computers. **Porches, street life and neighborhoods have been replaced by backyard patios, large screen televisions and the Internet.**

In *"The Long Tail",* author Chris Anderson writes about the effect of the internet on our society. Anderson writes,

"On-line today, we're doing different things, but we are more likely to encounter other individuals, either by reading their writings, chatting live, or just following their example. What we've lost in common culture we've made up in our increase exposure to other people."

I agree with most of this statement, and what I perceive to be the intent behind it. **We have lost the culture of interacting face to face and are rapidly moving to a global society of humans who live through their keyboard.** Anderson's comment about exposure to other people is totally true. Think of how many people you can reach out to through blogs, chat lines and "cc" lists on your computer or hand-held devices. But increased exposure is a double-edged sword. It obviously doesn't mean personally interacting with these other people. It means being exposed to a greater number of people. This form of impersonal exposure, in its own right, is becoming the new common culture. It's the willingness to forgo personal interaction for the ability to sit alone behind a computer screen. This lack of human interaction and touch is creating an "electronic culture."

Let me be clear. I don't want to have increased exposure to other people just for the sake of having that exposure, or if it requires me to have less face to face exposure and interaction with other human beings. If this is the case, then are we not raising an entire generation of computer literate and societal illiterates for the sake of expediency and the protection of our privacy? **In time, won't we become as much an extension to our electronic devices...as they are to us?** I'm not saying that our technological advances aren't saving us a lot of time. I love being out of the office or on the road and being able to pull out my Blackberry and dispatch 20 e-mails in no time flat. I love the effectiveness of voice-mails and I know that my overall efficiency has dramatically improved. It's the human element that appears to be suffering as we drive our technology forward.

In the 01/99 issue of *"The Harvard Business Review,"* Dr. Edward M. Hallowell, noted psychiatrist, teacher and author, writes about something he terms, *"The Human Moment at Work,"* stated as: *an authentic psychological encounter that can happen only when two people share the same physical space requiring people's physical presence and their emotional and Intellectual attention.* Dr. Hallowell cites numerous studies including the MacArthur Foundation study that all share similar findings.

Dr. Hallowell's article states that, *"the absence of the human moment in an organization can wreak havoc. Teams lose their sense of cohesiveness, people become distracted, distrusting, and* the culture will be riddled with anxiety, toxic worry and alienation." The doctor continues to discuss how technological advances (i.e. e-mail, voice mail etc) are increasingly limiting this human moment by "eliminating face time and removing cues (body language, facial expression, tone of voice) that come with being in an interpersonal vacuum."

With each computer up-grade our daily compassion for others deteriorates. **Why does it take a disaster of such devastating proportion for us to look up from our televisions, computers, I-Pods or Blackberries to see what is happening**. Why do we have to wait for earthquakes in China's Sichuan province, a Tsunami in Indonesia, or a Hurricane in the Southern States to wake up and feel the need to interact in a humane way and offer to help?

Where is the grace of how people interact with each other? Tell me that we shouldn't all be stepping up to the plate and trying to preserve elements that have made our society rich. How much further down the scale do we have to slide before there is no grace left between us?

We can't ignore what is happening to all of us through the influence of the press, music, the arts, the internet, movies, and reality television. We can't turn a blind eye to what is happening to our future generations in a school system hamstrung by budget constraints and archaic school board systems. The breakdown of the family unit is being underplayed, or worse, ignored. Each generation appears to becoming less gracious than the preceding one. Our society is suffering, as the next generation becomes engulfed in the intoxicating global lure of the Internet, music videos and out-right violence. **The basis of our culture is being torn apart.**

Comedian Steven Wright only half-heartedly jokes, "Support bacteria because they're the only culture some people have."

This is one of those overwhelming topics that seem to be insurmountable. So what can you personally do about it?

1. **Consider how you are treating your family and friends.** Do you treat them with the proper respect? Do you take them for granted or do you let them know how important they are to you with kind words and actions? Do you interact with them as you would if the Queen of England were sitting in the room? Do you treat non-family people better than you treat your family?

2. **Consider how you are conducting yourself outside of your house.** Do you drive like a maniac or do you conduct yourself with proper driving courtesy? Do you say hello to people on the street...even if you don't know them? Do you make an effort to get to know your neighbors? At work, do you treat everyone politely or just those in positions more senior than your own? Next time you come into contact at work with someone you don't know, stop and introduce yourself.

3. **Do you live on your key-board?** Go back to Chapter 2 and read about adventures and get the heck out of your house. Go do something!

4. **Are you providing your children the proper example** of how they should be interacting with each other, with you, and non-family members? They will emulate your actions...not your words. Are you monitoring: what they are doing on the computer; what

they are watching on the television; what electronic games they are play; and, who they talk about other kids?

5. **How are you interacting with people at your job?** Stop sending e-mails when a personal visit can help reduce the chance of misunderstanding because of the lack of human interface. Make sure you are seeing co-workers and customers face to face on a regular basis. Nothing can replace human interaction.

6. **Understand the role you play in society in helping to define our culture.** Every one of us has a part to play in how we either help bring our communities together...or keep them apart. Take a stand in what you are prepared to accept from broadcasters and the producers of DVDs and music that you find unacceptable for yourself, your children and for the welfare of our culture. Don't be an innocent bystander.

Chapter 35 Key:

It's not coincidental that societal breakdowns are occurring globally at the same pace that technology and the internet are gaining momentum. Neither can succeed in the future without the other. How do we return to our front-porches?

Chapter 36

"Study history, study history. In history lies all the secrets of statecraft..."

-Winston Churchill

I've learned more about anticipating the future by studying past events, than anything else I have ever done. If you want to better anticipate what might be coming your way, turn around and look behind you. I'm constantly amazed at how many people repeat actions expecting a different and more successful outcome. This applies to their career choices, relationships, health decisions and business investments. If you want a different outcome, you have to take a different course of action. The same theory applies to Politicians. How many times must mistakes be repeated before our Politicians learn "the truths" from their history lessons?

There was an incredible reaction to Al Gore's *"Inconvenient Truth,"* yet the truths of which he speaks are not new. **Perhaps truths have to be discussed for decades before people actually pay attention.**

Let me put the theme of this chapter into context by sharing a story about a dear friend of mine: George Washington Adams is the most eclectic person I have ever known. He is widower with five marriages under his belt. George was born in Buffalo, New York and attributes his great wealth and health to fresh air, lots of sleep, good hydration, steady exercise, his adventurous "spark," and as much sex as he can muster. George has fathered twenty-four children who gave him sixty-five grandchildren, who in turn bore twenty-two great grandchildren. Oh yes, last March, George turned 124 years old. He was born in 1884. Of course this is hard to accept...so read on.

When he turned thirteen years old, George Adams ran away from home to join the hordes of gold-seeking adventurers striking out for the Yukon. After making the horrific trek to Dawson City, George won a poker hand and a small mining stake from a Swede who had recently immigrated from the old country. The mining stake was on the now famous Bonanza Creek. Two days after arriving at his claim, George Adams waded out into the creek where something caught his eye. Reaching down into the cold water near a half-submerged tree trunk, he pulled out a golf-ball sized nugget of 24 karat gold. Then he saw another. By the end of that day, he collected more than a hundred pounds of gold nuggets from beneath that log. Two months later he left the Klondike an incredibly wealthy young man of thirteen. He spent the next five years travelling across the States wondering how to spend his new-found wealth.

In 1905, George returned to Buffalo and married his child-hood sweetheart. Sarah immediately provided him with children, and a loving house. As he thought about the rest of his life and how to spend his money, George studied the world events in progress and the history that had led up to it. He realized that the globe was going to explode with growth and opportunity. George's father told him to study history and learn how to anticipate where, and how, those opportunities would arise. Even as a young man, he saw that there were parallels in the early 1900s to earlier times.

"This growth revolution in the USA is like England one hundred years ago," he told Sarah. "When that occurred, investors understood the importance of transporting people and goods. They turned to the steam engine which in trains required steel and coal. The engine also created factories which needed bricks, steel, mortar, wood and a workforce. This drew families to the cities and they needed housing and hospitals. The production of finished materials opened up avenues of exporting that the world had never seen. Transportation of those goods became paramount."

Behind this theory, George invested most of his fortune in trains, oil and steel. Through friends, he met and invested behind a man named Ford and something being termed an "assembly line." Communication of information seemed to be holding back business from its full potential. The telegraph was still in use but the telephone was becoming the communication vehicle of the future. Interested in the communication and exchange of information, he placed a small fortune in a new company called the Computing Tabulating Recording Corporation in 1916. It was listed as CTR but changed its name eight years later...to IBM. George continued to travel across the States seeking opportunities. He invested another fortune in Texas seeking black gold. Again, he wouldn't be disappointed and his oil fields soon supplied the black liquid to more than a fifteen percent of the entire country.

As the decades passed, his interests grew more global in nature. His net worth surpassed a billion dollars before he turned forty. George built munitions plants that supplied the armed forces in every war during the 20th Century.

When asked about his success over the years, George consistently replied that his business and investing philosophy was simple.

"If you want to find opportunities in the future, simply understand your history books. Find analogies in different times and places and you can become an incredibly successful prognosticator."

In 1965, George celebrated his 80th birthday, only days after his 5th wife Victoria had succumbed to liver cancer. He sold all of their houses and bought a "retirement village," which was refurbished to the standards of the Four Seasons' Hotel in London. With Victoria's passing, he decided to dramatically step up his efforts of "giving back." In her memory, he donated $250 million to Cancer Research. After this initial donation, he created the "Klondike River Foundation" to build hospitals, and to provide research grants to medical institutions. Over the last four decades George Adam's foundation has issued over $1.5 Billion of grants towards medical care, research and hospital improvements on every continent.

The other week, I visited George at his home in the village. He maintains and houses a live-in cook, maid, full-time nurse, secretarial assistant, and a gentleman's gentleman, named Chester Sanford. I'd guess his gentleman's gentleman is close to 85 years. Chester spends a lot of the day sleeping in a large winged-back leather chair just inside the vestibule. As is the custom, George greeted me at the door, told me not to disturb Chester, and handed me a steaming cup of Ovaltine. The smell of the dark foamy liquid invaded my nostrils and instantly cleared my sinuses.

"Drink this while it's hot," George directed, as he turned and shuffled off towards the kitchen. George's private rooms are over 8,000 square feet, but he spends the most time at the kitchen table, or studying his investments at a nearby desk which is cluttered with paper and books.

"You know this stuff is absolutely revolting," I replied, knowing my opinion would fall on deaf ears-literally.

George sat down at the kitchen table and picked up a J-Cloth. He began cleaning out the inside of the now-empty Ovaltine tin. I joined him and sat quietly until he carefully inspected the empty tin ensuring it was pristine. Curiously, I watched as he picked up a box of pills and placed it inside the tin. I saw the word "Viagra" printed on the side of the box.

"Okay, I'm stumped," I admitted, poking at the tin with my right index finger. George smiled, and leaned forward as if to whisper to me.

"It's one thing having everyone in my family know that I use Preparation-H and Metamucil. It's another for them to see the box of Viagra," he muttered, as he replaced the lid on the Ovaltine container. "I do have a reputation to protect you know."

"So George, how often to you use Viagra?" I asked, hoping for a limited answer and no elaboration or details.

"Every second day," he answered shortly, and I breathed a sigh of relief at the brevity of his response. Fortunately for me, George felt no need to elaborate.

I took a sip of my Ovaltine. My stomach immediately braced itself and a gurgle wended its way through my lower intestines. It was time to change the subject.

"How's the blog coming today?" I asked, knowing that George loved discussing his blog. He spent two hours each morning cobbling together his thoughts on the world. On average, a hundred thousand people logged on daily to try to gain learning, and free investment tips from George Adams.

"I think it's pretty good today," he replied, as he looked out the window to see who was walking about the perfectly landscaped centre courtyard. As he stared, he reached up and took out his upper dentures.

With his left hand, he re-opened the can of Ovaltine holding his box of Viagra. He slipped the dentures inside the can and then replaced the lid. I didn't bother to ask why. Every action George carried out had a very deliberate purpose. He looked up at me.

"What were we talking about anyway?"

"We were talking about your blog. What was the topic today?" I asked. I was having a little difficulty understand George who tended to lisp when his dentures were out.

"I ranted on for a while about how today's political leaders are in desperate need to crack open their history books to learn a thing or two about what's going on today in the world. I think watching a few good movies might help them to stop making so many stupid decisions. It's like they don't understand that most things happening today have already happened before. **Why don't today's politicians learn from the past**? I've said the same thing every time I've met a President, Prime-Minister or dictator since 1915. Actually, it's not just politicians who should be learning from history…it's everyone."

"Give me an example," I asked, grateful to see the bottom of my empty cup of Ovaltine. My insides were in full revolt and I steeled myself for the pending attack I would have to face.

George took out his comb and ran it through his full head of white hair. On any given day, he reminded me of Spencer Tracey with all that white hair.

"Alright," George replied. "Let's play a game. Throw out some event of great importance that comes to your mind."

I didn't hesitate very long before blurting out, "9/11."

George nodded. "How heartbreaking that was. Unfortunately, we should have seen this coming. The method of attack has been used many times before with even greater numbers of fatalities. Let's see…a combatant using a vessel filled with fuel to attack an enemy. Off the top of my head I remember WWII and the Kamikaze suicide planes attacking Pearl Harbor; the USS Hancock; the USS Intrepid; and, a number of other ships in the Pacific. In WWII, the German Luftwaffe had volunteer suicide missions using their airplanes to attack bridge fortifications near Hannover and on the Oder River in Russia. Heck, if I remember my history lessons, the Medievel Crusaders used a number of suicide ships laden with explosives to attack a Muslim fortress. This methodology of attack is not new. It *appeared* new in a time when CNN and the Internet could display exact film footage as the attacks occurred. I think that's really the only difference. I think people got lazy and weren't paying enough attention to what they should have been."

"Okay," I responded, "Talk to me about CEOs who have imprisoned for breaching financial rules. This seems to have reached epidemic proportions. Any experience in history about that?"

"You're referring to the likes of Worldcom's Bernard Ebbers, Enron's Jeffery Skilling, Computer Associates' Sanjay Kumar, Conrad Black and Martha Stewart?"

"Exactly," I answered.

"Well, let's remember Michael Milken—the Junk Bond king of the 80s; Foster Winans who wrote for the Wall Street Journal and shared advanced details of his business column with pals; or maybe Carlo Ponzi who ran afoul of the Securities Exchange Commission for fraudulent pyramid schemes back in the 1920's. I almost got sucked in on that one myself. Do you remember why Capone went to jail? Income tax evasion. Again the difference today is the power of the Internet and the press to bring the issues quickly to the forefront. There has always been fraud and racketeering and there always will be. The SEC has been given more power, in part, because of the high visibility of the Internet and the media."

"Not bad...I've got a few more for you," I continued, wanting to test his memory.

George looked at his watch and shook his head.

"I can't keep playing this game right now. I need to take my pills. You go over to the computer and read my blog and then we'll talk about it."

George reached beneath the kitchen table and pulled up a large Nike sports bag. Unzipping it, he withdrew a brown leather-covered journal and around 30 boxes and plastic containers of pills. I had watched this routine before. Five times daily George had to take fifteen different pills, each in a certain order. He was meticulous about the routine and in documenting his actions in the brown journal. I got up from the table and walked over to his desk. Photos of his family adorned the desk amongst the piles of unopened envelopes containing letters from strangers asking for money and donations. His desktop computer was buried somewhere in the middle. I cleared a path and found his keyboard. I typed in the password and looked back to see George fingering a large orange pill the size of a small chipmunk.

"God Almighty George," I squawked. "Do you take that all at once?

He smiled back at grinned. "That's why I had to take out my uppers." He laughed as he chucked the pill into his mouth and grimaced painfully, as he swallowed. I returned to look at his blog that now filled the screen.

Why today's politicians should pay attention to what's already happened before so they can avoid repeating the same mistakes made by other idiot politicians.

By George Washington Adams, June, 2008.

First of all, remember that I am 124 years old and was born in 1884. I know what I am talking about because I've been around. I've lived through 24 Presidents of the United States and 22 Prime Ministers of Canada. The Civil War ended fourteen years before my mother went into labor with me. Hell, my father, Benjamin Franklin Adams fought at Little Round Top with Colonel Chamberlain and helped the Union win Gettysburg. I'm a very old man and I've seen a lot in my life. So listen up and pay attention.

I'm fed up with the same mistakes being repeated by politicians. It's the same the world over. In particular, I'm fed up with watching our boys and girls die in wars. I'm not saying whether invading Afghanistan or Iraq was right or wrong. That's no longer the issue. What is the issue is that we need to get our kids out of Iraq and Afghanistan right now. Not tomorrow and not next year: Right now. It does not matter anymore about saving face or the longevity political parties holding power. We cannot be held hostage by body-bag-backed rhetoric of "exit strategies." Our children are dying. Get them out. Why didn't the pants-creased Generals and knee-jerk politicians look to the history of Iraq and Afghanistan before they pulled the trigger? Have none of them studied previous invasions of those countries by the Romans, the Crusaders and Great Britain? Each invasion failed miserably and the Brits learned a brutal lesson as recently as *ninety years ago*. Tell me if anything sounds familiar today from what England surmised after their disastrous invasion was called off:

1. The British realized that they didn't send in enough troops to "rectify the problem they wished to fix." Public sentiment didn't support the invasion and the politicians hummed and hawed trying to figure out how best not to lose the next election. While they did, British soldiers were dying every day.

2. The British admitted that they hadn't planned an exit strategy, nor did they anticipate how formidable the enemy would be.

3. The British soldiers faced daily ambushes, road side attacks, guerilla warfare and bombs. They had trouble finding the enemy who had no trouble finding them.

And as for Afghanistan, perhaps our military geniuses could have consulted their history books and learned that invaders launching into Afghanistan have always come out of the short end of the stick. Anyone ever heard of Alexander the Great; the British expedition; or even the USSR invasion in the early 1980s? Simple lesson in warfare: you can't fight an enemy you can't find when the terrain is his ally.

Why didn't someone in charge read a history book?

For a change in pace, let's move off war-fare and discuss something that is also affecting everyone. Part 2 of today's blog is about "oil." We've been here before if you look at you history books back to the 1970s. Working families can't afford to pay these artificially-induced prices...and the earth's oil supply can't sustain the abhorrent demands we're placing on it.

Experts tell us these facts:

1. We're using too much oil. Now there's an MBA for you. Anyone consider how much more oil is about to be used to propel the

explosive industrial growth in India and China over the next twenty-five to fifty years? Can you imagine the investment opportunities required to put those infrastructures in place? Would sure help to speak the language, wouldn't it?

2. World demand has outreached capacity and oil producers haven't made the investment to improve upon that capacity. How intentional was this?

3. Instability and the threat of wars add pressure to oil-producing nations. We've seen this in print in each of the last eight decades. When has there ever been sustained peace in the Middle East or African nations like Nigeria?

These are the same facts that experts reeled off almost forty years ago. Look at news clippings from 4-5 decades ago. I will admit that there are some differences. For example, we might want to be reconsidering the number of cars and trucks on the road; and, the number, and size of airplanes in the sky. Here's the logic flow as history will tell us: Instability...threat of violence or disruption to oil "balance"...someone invades someplace...oil prices sky rocket...defense industry booms...the automotive industry tanks...auto-related industries are collateral damage...the airline industry takes a bath...jobs are lost...mortgages can't be paid...crime rises...currencies decline...gold price goes up...the global stock markets takes a hit...the economy enters that horrible "R-word" and then someone decides it's time for a larger land-war to kick the whole cycle back into gear by stabilizing the oil "balance." How many times must we allow this cycle to repeat itself?

But there is another factor I want you to consider from history. It's also the reality in times like this, that **while many are facing severe financial pressures, others are making a lot of money.** For the last century **whenever too few people are controlling too much money, something seriously wrong happens**. Throughout history we've been in these periods of imbalance and the long-term effects are damaging. Plutarch wrote, "*Imbalance between rich and poor is the oldest and most fatal ailment of all Republics.*" Look at the collapse of the Roman Empire, 1800s France, 1900 Russia and most recently, the Soviet Union. And now, like so many times throughout our history, we have too few people controlling the world's supply of oil. The recipe is one of disaster for the economy and foundations of any industrial nation.

―――――――――――――

Sitting back in my chair, I reflected upon George's blog. Not bad for a 124 year old man. **History does have a way of repeating itself and it you study your history it can't but help you better face the future.** I glanced up and saw a small wooden plaque handing on the wall directly in front of George's desk.

"History, despite its wrenching pain, cannot be unlived, but if faced with courage, need not be lived again..."

-Maya Angelou

The doorbell sounded and when I glanced over Chester was still leaning heavily into his deep winged-back chair...sound asleep. I walked over to the door, opened it, and was greeted with the warmest smile and the loveliest bright green eyes.

"Hello. I'm Virginia. Mr. Adams is expecting me."

Virginia was a fetching woman in her mid-60s, with a full figure and a lightening bright smile. She looked like Ellen Burstyn and was fashionably-dressed in a light blue pant suit which accentuated her figure.

"Hi Virginia, I'm Howard and I'll tell George you're here. Won't you please come in?"

Virginia smiled and walked through the door. She stepped over Chester's out-stretched legs and gently patted him on the left cheek. As if out of habit, she placed her purse on the table immediately inside the vestibule. She looked into the small round mirror and checked her teeth for lipstick. I was about to inquire how she knew my friend when he appeared directly behind me.

"Good, I see you two have met," George said, with a huge grin, rubbing his hands together. "Here you are two of my favorite people standing in one room." He turned to his visitor and asked, "How are you Ginny? Get a good sleep last night?"

"Well I'm just perfect George," she smiled, and cocked her head sideways. "You all ready?"

"Sure am," he replied eagerly.

Virginia giggled, as my stomach turned. Was it the discomfort of listening to this conversation or the Ovaltine finally eating through the wall of my stomach?

"Time for me to go," I said aloud, but no one heard.

I reached for my coat and bent over to pick up my briefcase. George had his arm around Virginia's waist and they were headed down the hallway like a pair of teenagers. As I opened the door, I glanced back. Virginia had entered the bedroom and as George turned to close the door, he smiled and winked at me.

I returned the wink, walked past the sleeping Chester and got the hell out of there as fast as my Ovaltine-laden stomach would allow.

Chapter 36 Key:

The future is as uncertain as the past. Look for clues from times gone by in your own life, and throughout the history of civilization. These clues can help you to prepare and invest your time, energies and finances accordingly. Become a student of history and you will become a teacher of the future. Don't just stand on the side-lines.

Epilogue:

I hope something in **"A page from a CEO's Diary"** touches you. For over 30 years, I've had the benefit of some of the best examples of leadership, and mentoring, that a person could hope to have. I thank all of those wonderful leaders who helped me through their words of wisdom and example.

Remember this: **You have within you the ability to be much more than you are today**. You owe it to your family, your friends and your co-workers to "be your best." You owe it to your community and to your country. But above all, **you owe it to yourself to be the best person you can be**. Life is not a dress rehearsal and there's no *do-over*.

If you completed Chapter 1's exercise you have a better understanding of who you are and who you wish to be. I hope you formulated a game-plan to help make this transition in words and actions. If you did, all of this will unfold naturally as long as you understand that you can't go it alone. **We all need others to help us achieve our goals in our career, and our lives**. This is not a game to be played alone. **The caliber of the team-mates you play with will determine your ultimate success.**

There will be unforeseen blocks and obstacles thrown at you every day. **How successfully you maneuver roadblocks and frustrations is the true sign of your character.** In particular, don't play ostrich if you are in a job you detest; have a boss who is an idiot; or, have bullies wreaking havoc with you, or yours. Don't ignore the vital role that persistence will play in your overcoming any of these obstacles. I can't stress enough that **you need to find "life guides" to help you along the way.** And never under-estimate that **you control your finances and use of time no matter what is happening around you, or to you.**

From this day forward, be sure to go **at life in such a way that you are forced to be your best by stretching yourself to your physical, mental and emotional limits. Find adventures in everything you do.**

Please take care to find the balance between technology and ideas. **Our world is desperate for ideas**...not just the next version of software, a faster computer or a phone that does everything but walk the dog. And remember that **almost everything that will come at us in the future has, in some way, come at our ancestors before us**. The rub is in finding the connection.

I've enjoyed sharing **"*A page from a CEO's Diary*"** and hope you took away a lesson or two. Tell your friends about this book which can be ordered at: **www.authorhouse.com**

Remember that in the first two years of publication, all of my net proceeds from the sale of this book will be divided equally between Camp Oochigeas and PrevNet. **We are our brother's keeper.**

Enjoy this day and tell the people you love what they mean to you.

-Howard J. Breen, September, 2008

Bibliography And Recommended Reading

Adams, Michael. *Fire and Ice: The United States, Canada and the Myth of Converging Values*. Toronto, Canada: Penguin Group. 2003.

Anderson, Chris. *The Long Tail: Why the Future of Business is Selling Less of More*. New York: Hyperion. 2006.

Beckworth, Harvey. *Selling the Invisible*. New York: Warner Books. 1997.

Braudel, Fernand. *The Perspective of the World: Civilization and Capitalism in the 15th-18th Century*. William Collins Sons & Co. Ltd. and Harper & Row, Publishers, Inc. 1984.

Carlson, Richard. *Don't Sweat the Small Stuff*. New York: Hyperion. 1997.

Collis, James C., and Jerry I. Porras. *Built to last: Successful Habits of Visionary Companies*. New York: HarperBusiness, 1994.

Covey, Stephen. *The 7 Habits of Highly Effective People: Powerful Lessons in Personal Change*. New York: Simon & Schuster Publishing. 1987.

D'Adamo, Peter J., with Catharine Whitney. *Eat Right For Your Blood Type*. New York. G.P. Putnam's sons Publishing. 1996.

Dalla Costa, John. *The Ethical Imperative: Why Moral Leadership is Good Business*. Reading Massachusetts: Addison Wesley Longman, Inc. 1998.

DePree, Max. *Leadership Is an Art*. New York: Bantam Doubleday Dell, 1989.

Friedman, Thomas L. *The Lexus And The Olive Tree: Understanding Globalization.* New York: Farrar, Straus and Giroux. 1990.

Friedman, Thomas L. *The World is Flat*: *A Brief History of the Twenty-First Century*. New York: Farrar, Straus and Giroux. 2005.

Funny quotes, sayings, useful maxims @ : http://www.businessballs. com/quotes.htm

Gaines-Ross, Leslie. *CEO Capital: A Guide to Building CEO Reputation and Company Success.* New Jersey: John Wiley & Sons. 2003.

Galbraith, John Kenneth. *The Anatomy of Power*. Boston: Houghton Mifflin, 1983.

Gore, Al. *The Assault on Reason*. New York: Penguin Group USA. 2007.

Hagstrom, Robert G. *The Warren Buffet Way: Investment Strategies of the World's Greatest Investor*. New York. John Wiley & Sons. 1994.

Hagstrom, Robert G. *The Essential Buffet: Timeless Principles for the New Economy.* New York. John Wiley& Sons.2001.

Hallowell, Edward M. *The Human Moment at Work*. Harvard Business Review Reprint 99104. Original January-February, 1999.

Hawking, Stephen. *The Universe in a Nutshell*. New York: Bantam Books, a Division of Random House. 2001.

Holtz, Lou. *Winning Every Day: The Game Plan for Success*. New York: HarperCollins Publishers Inc. 1998.

Iacocca, Lee. Novak, William. *Iacocca.* New York. Randon House Publishing. 1986.

Kanderstag Declaration Against Bullying in children and youth @ www. ncab.org.au/pdfs/Kanderstag%20Declaration.pdf

Krashinsky,Susan. *What to do about cyber bullies? Get real, for a start..* Globe and Mail, Division of CTVglobemedia. May 15, 2008.

Lawrence, T.E. *Seven Pillars of Wisdom*. New York: Doubleday, Doran & Company, Inc. 1935.

Lewis, Michael. *Moneyball: The Art of Winning an Unfair Game*. New York: W.W. Norton & Company, Inc. 2003.

Llewellyn, Richard. *How Green was my Valley*. New York. Penguin Publishing. 1939.

Lucas, James R. *Balance of Power*. New York: AMACOM, 1998.

Moore, James F. *The Death of Competition: Leadership & Strategy in the Age of Business Ecosystems*. New York: HarperCollins Publishers, Inc. 1996.

Pepler, Debra J and Craig, Wendy. *Making a Difference in Bullying*; Report #60 @www.arts.yorku.ca/lamarsh/pdf/Making_a_Difference_in_Bullying/pdf

Powell, Colin with Joseph E. Persico. *My American Journey*. New York: Random House. 1995.

Quittner, Josh. *The Lessons of Amazon.com's Jeff Bezos*. Fortune 500. May 5, 2008.

Ries, Al. *Focus: The Future of Your Company Depends on It*. New York: HarperBusiness, 1996.

Sears, Barry. *Mastering the Zone*. New York: HarperCollins Publishers, Inc. 1997.

Shank, Roger. *The Creative Attitude: Learning to Ask and Answer the Right Questions*. New York: MacMillan Publishing Company. 1998.

Siklos, Richard. *Interview with Bob Iger, CEO Disney*. New York. Fortune Magazine. April, 2008.

Slater, Robert. *Jack Welch and the GE Way*. New York. McGraw-Hill. 2000.

Stanford News Service. *You've got to find what you love, Jobs says*. Text of Steve Jobs Commencement Address (2005). http://news-service.stanford.edu/news/2005/june15/jobs-061505.html

Stanley, Thomas J., and William D. Danko. *The Millionaire Next Door*. Marietta Georgia: Longstreet Press Inc. 1996.

Stengel, Richard. *Nelson Mandella*: *8 Lessons of Leadership*. New York. Time Magazine. July, 2008.

Von Clausewitz, Carl. *On War.* First published in 1832. Abridge Version New York: Barnes & Noble: London, Routeledge & Kegan Paul. 1996.

About The Author:

Howard J. Breen is the Chairman and Chief Executive Officer of one of Canada's largest and pre-eminent Advertising and Communication Companies. His career spans 30+ years in Canada and the USA. He serves as Director on numerous business, and charitable Boards. He lives in Toronto, Canada with his wife Martha, their two teenage children, and their Airedale Ginger.

LaVergne, TN USA
31 August 2009
156548LV00001B/16/P